Praise for *Recipe for Business Success*

"Dan has an insatiable desire for knowledge and understanding of best business practices, and an even greater desire to share his knowledge and wisdom with others. In *Recipe for Business Success,* Dan incorporates all his learnings into a HOW-TO summary. Dan's wisdom to acknowledge and express that no two businesses are alike enables the reader to feel comfortable with their own model, while assessing the highest, best value for everyone's learning needs. We agree that *Recipe for Business Success* is a must read for business leaders to realize the significance of the convergence of Culture, Strategy, and Execution."

Lisa and Barry Allen, former CEO and Chief People Officer, Ziegenfelder Company

"Seeing the knowledge and wisdom my team at ASCEND and I have absorbed over the years as part of an easy-to-digest book makes me excited for the growth and success that any reader and their organization are likely to see. Whether you are at the helm of a multi-national enterprise or a scrappy, local non-profit, Dan's recipe is surely one to follow."

Alex Bernstein, Co-Founder, ASCEND Summit LLC

"I have had the pleasure and benefit of knowing Dan Adley as a mentor, board member, and as a guide in developing our organization's strategic plan. As the CEO of a midsize organization, I can confidently say that his approach produces superior results while being sensitive to the limited resources and challenges that smaller organizations face. Dan's direct, clear style with vivid examples makes this book one that every leader of small to midsize organizations should study."

Bob Chalker, CAE; CEO, Association for Material Protection and Performance

"The underlying concepts set forth in *Recipe for Business Success* are based on a number of business management theories set forth in complex works most often written by academics and large public company advisors and managers, limiting their usefulness to the management teams of small and medium-sized privately-held businesses and other smaller entities. Dan does an exceptional job of reducing these important and meaningful theories to a more understandable and targeted level, thereby providing an easy to utilize roadmap for managers and owners of these entities."

Robert J. Grossman CPA, MS, CVA; Co-Founder/Partner,
Grossman Yanak&Ford, Tax & Business Valuation Services

"In *Recipe for Business Success*, Dan Adley takes a unique approach to defining an organization's success to be much more than merely making money or funding a non-profit's initiative. Adley highlights a non-financial concept, Culture, as a key piece in the foundation to defining one's 'success.' The Culture of an organization is the glue that keeps the organization on track towards its goals through good and not so good times. Along with Culture, Adley mixes in Strategy and Execution, the more traditional components of Success in a step by step and understandable way. Adley then takes the Success recipe and applies it in the real-world example of ASCEND Summit LLC. A wonderful read of 'how to' make your organization focus and realize Success."

John M. Lally, CPA, MBA, CVA; Founder, Lally &
Co., LLC, CPAs and Business Advisors

"At some point in time a leader interested in growing their business realizes they need a solid strategic plan. This book simplifies and amplifies the path one would choose to take as they set course on their journey to growth and greatness.

Jim Landino, Founder and CEO, JCL Energy

"Having the privilege of leading the employee-owned business that was the breeding ground for much of the content of this book, I can whole heartedly recommend it to those leaders of small to mid-sized enterprises looking for a practical and scalable approach to guiding their organizations to success. Dan's imprint on the culture and success of KTA-Tator is a testament to his passion, knowledge and commitment to the principles expounded in *Recipe for Business Success.*"

David McFayden, CEO, KTA-Tator, Inc.

"Dan is an exemplar of living in the intersection of the three spaces he so superbly describes in his book. There are no half measures in what he sets out to do, such as completing a marathon in all 50 states, which he did at a marathon in Napa, CA that I personally witnessed. His book has my whole-hearted endorsement."

Arvind Paranjpe, President-Dynamic Leadership,
Ltd.; Chair Emeritus Vistage Worldwide

"Having been familiar with Dan for several years, it is a pleasure to have a book from an author that has not only practiced what he is now preaching, but has implemented to an exceptionally high level."

Robert J. Powell, Founder & CEO, Invictus Leadership
Group; Chair, Vistage Worldwide

"Dan Adley has written a thoughtful analysis of how to develop a great culture and an effective strategic planning process. It's not filled with platitudes, but rather nuts-and-bolts tools you can use to help your company define its mission and vision and achieve them."

Corey Rosen, PhD; Author; Founder, National
Center for Employee Ownership

"FINALLY – A business primer that consolidates all essential ingredients for success in a single resource for time-challenged managers of small and mid-sized organizations."

Amy Veltri, Founder and CEO, NGE Consulting

Recipe for
BUSINESS
SUCCESS

Recipe for
BUSINESS
SUCCESS

Getting the Right Mix of
CULTURE, STRATEGY, AND EXECUTION

DANIEL P. ADLEY

Author – Daniel P. Adley
Editorial & Publishing Assistance – Eland Mann
Design & Graphics – G Sharp Design, LLC – George B. Stevens
Distribution of the first edition (2023) – Ingram Book Group

ISBN: 979-8-9871363-3-1 (paperback)
ISBN: 979-8-9871363-4-8 (e-book)

To my wife Joan, our children and extended family,
and the many mentors, peers, and friends
who have influenced and supported me throughout my career.
I owe you all my undying gratitude.

PREFACE

Two friends who shared an entrepreneurial spirit and deep love of rock climbing began envisioning the first-of-its-kind, integrated indoor climbing and fitness experience in Pittsburgh. ASCEND would be a local pioneer, providing top-tier indoor rock climbing combined with aligned training facilities linked with outdoor climbing excursions and programming to accommodate and engage novice through expert climbers.

Original cofounders Alex Bernstein and Paul Guarino were joined by Aaron Gilmore as the three-person management team that sought and secured initial funding. A Board of Managers (BoM) that included the three founders and several initial investors helped guide the development and launch of ASCEND Pittsburgh in January 2017. The founders quickly developed the business practices necessary to service a growing clientele, and ASCEND Pittsburgh was operating profitably within the first year of operation.

With this initial growth and success, by early 2018, the BoM identified the need to formalize longer-term goals and strategies. As a member of the board, an investor, and a great supporter of the founders, I volunteered to help guide the effort and facilitate their strategic planning.

I'm a scientist by education and experience, but my passion for learning emerged from other areas of exploration in leadership in general, and business management specifically. When I entered the workforce in the late '70s, I was introduced to Management by Objectives (MBO), the form of planning outlined in Peter Drucker's *Practice of Management* (1954). Later I was influenced by W. Edwards Deming's *Out of Crisis* (1982*).* As I broadened my perspective and became a fervent practitioner of strategic planning in varying forms, I applied its concepts to aspects of my personal, professional, and business life. And as I grew in proficiency, opportunities emerged as a facilitator of the strategic planning process for other for-profit and not-for-profit organizations.

In addition to a passion for strategic planning, I have carried a trait for lifelong learning with me throughout my career, supplementing formal training in my chosen profession with reasonably extensive reading of business books and journals, attending seminars, listening to audible courses, and participating monthly in Vistage, an executive peer group, for over fifteen years. I learned a lot from these authors and lecturers but came to realize that much of what is written is developed by, and even for, big business.

Executives of large companies fill the covers of magazines, and their books dominate available space at the local bookstore. Coverage of large businesses consumes the business news. There is nothing inherently wrong with this, and in fact much can be gained from careful consideration of the perspectives of such great thought leaders. But the ideas and recommended practices aimed at large, publicly traded businesses do not readily translate to small and mid-sized companies, at least not without considerable effort.

Small and mid-sized for-profit businesses are the epitome of what keeps America going. And this says nothing about the countless not-for-profit organizations, professional and charitable associations, academic institutions, and governmental agencies that face similar business challenges.

The ideas and recommended practices aimed at large, publicly traded businesses do not readily translate to small and mid-sized companies, at least not without considerable effort.

For decades, one question has guided my work: *How can large, corporate strategic management practices be best applied to small, entrepreneurial startup-like organizations?*

On a personal basis, I believe it is necessary to have a core purpose to live a meaningful and fulfilling life. My personal Why is "To help improve the lives of others." Friends, peers, people I've worked with, and leadership of professional associations I've had the pleasure to engage with, suggested I write about the integrated, intentional business practices I've found to be essential ingredients to success.

At the risk of great hubris, and in recognition of the need for intellectual humility, I set out to distill and consolidate in an actionable format a "recipe for business success" for small and mid-size organizations of all forms. This book has emerged from a combination of lifelong learning and forty-five years of diverse business experience, including leading the transition of a second generation, family-owned business to a 100 percent employee-owned nationwide engineering services corporation with a 22 percent CAGR in share value over the ensuing ten years.

My hope is that *Recipe for Business Success*:

- removes distractions from the noise of big-business focused literature,
- challenges existing paradigms on leading successful organizations,
- focuses attention on three essential ingredients to success,
- offers actionable takeaways, and
- contributes to readers' individual and organizational success.

In that spirit, I share throughout the book the story of one such organization—the Pittsburgh-based rock-climbing provider, ASCEND Summit LLC—to illustrate the *Recipe for Business Success* process in practice for a small, entrepreneurial and highly successful startup company. In my role as strategic facilitator, I was fortunate to apply much of what's covered in this book to ASCEND's culture, strategy, and execution. By the end of 2022, ASCEND had not only survived 2 years of Covid-induced state-mandated shutdowns and occupancy restrictions, but opened a 3rd full service climbing facility and laid the foundations for their 4th facility in the regional market.

If you're a leader in a small or mid-sized organization, I hope *Recipe for Business Success* helps you address your most important business challenges in a systematic, sustainable manner for long-term success.

TABLE OF CONTENTS

PROLOGUE

What would be on your list if you were asked to "make a list as long as necessary but as short as possible of what it takes to be successful in business"? A quick internet search on "Keys to Success in Business" provides an indication of the types of items that might be on your list:

Quality products or services	Excellent staff	Well-designed website
Effective social media presence	Well organized	High employee retention
Great customer focus	Consistency	Competitive analysis
Judging risks and rewards	Creativity	Personal sacrifices
Problem-solving	Detailed processes	Etc., etc., etc.

The list could certainly go on much longer. But the challenge of the task was to make the list "…as long as necessary but as short as possible." In this somewhat contrived exercise, it is likely that nearly every response could reasonably be placed within one of three barrels labeled:

Culture   **Strategy**   **Execution**

wherein:

- **Culture** represents the values, systems, attitudes, and set of assumptions that people in an organization share and adopt to achieve stated goals and objectives.
- **Strategy** is the art and science of deploying resources (people, time, money) to achieve stated goals of the organization (i.e., enterprise, business unit, or product/service line).
- **Execution** involves having the right people required to support the organization's strategy and making sure they are efficiently doing what is most important to achieve stated goals.

A more thoughtful exercise might first start with creating a definition of success. What constitutes "success" in business? A quick internet search on "metrics for success in business" provides listings of the traditional metrics that might be tracked to evaluate the success of a business:

- general financial metrics related to sales, costs, and investments, or more specific financial outcomes like earnings growth, cash flow growth, and return on invested capital.
- nonfinancial measures such as customer loyalty, customer satisfaction, customer and employee retention, and product quality are also frequently cited.

Naturally, financial metrics can't capture all measures of success. But even the nonfinancial metrics are all outcome based. They reflect the end results. What about the broader purpose of a business?

While there are many competing and overlapping definitions of success in business, for the purposes of this book*, the definition of "Success" of a business (i.e., to fulfill its broader purpose), is:

> A successful corporation conducts a lawful, ethical, profitable, and sustainable business to grow value for all stakeholders over the long term while embracing environmental, social, and governance responsibilities.[1,2]

As we will be using this definition to define the end goal of our *Recipe for Business Success*, let's take a moment to unpack it. To be successful, every enterprise must operate profitably and be sustainable over the long haul while growing value for its stakeholders. This applies to both for-profit and not-for-profit organizations. The stakeholders may include but are not limited to investors, employees, customers, members, vendors, benefactors and beneficiaries, local communities, and society and the economy at large. Business success also requires stewardship over environmental, social, and governance responsibilities. The overarching goal of our Recipe for Business Success is to fulfill the aspirational statement of purpose outlined above.

With this definition of "Success" in mind, our recipe can be expressed as:

Success = Culture + Strategy + Execution

---

* | This definition is modified from the concept described in a September 17, 2020 post by Martin Lipton on the Harvard Law School Forum on Corporate Governance titled The Friedman Essay and the True Purpose of the Business Corporation

As indicated, the Recipe for Business Success we will explore is applicable to both for-profit and not-for-profit enterprises. But like any cookbook, the recipes are not for everyone. Without putting too fine a point on it, the business processes outlined in our Recipe for Business Success will be of greatest value:

By type of enterprise

Any business, professional and charitable association, academic institution, municipal or governmental agency wherein maintaining a desired culture, implementing effective strategies, and executing efficiently to accomplished identified goals is desired.

By type of ownership

Both for-profit and not-for-profit organizations that are oriented towards sustainably growing value for all stakeholders over the long term. As such, Recipe for Business Success may not be on point for those publicly traded, private equity owned, privately held, or other enterprises whose primary focus is on achieving short term results. On the other hand, it is particularly applicable for employee-owned companies as the recommended processes align well with participatory management, an engaged workforce, and long-term goals like accrual of wealth that are essential elements of employee ownership.

By size of organization

The processes outlined in Recipe for Business Success are most suitable for all but the two smallest classes (i.e., 1-4 and 5-9 employees) and the two largest (i.e., 500-999 and 1,000 or more) of 9 classes used by the Department of Labor. While the foundational information may be worthwhile, the complexity of the practices as described herein are likely to be unnecessarily challenging for the smallest of businesses, and additional development and oversight elements not addressed in this text may be necessary for the largest of businesses. That said, I have used elements of this recipe with a start-up not-for-profit association with no employees, and in establishing strategic direction and culture for the safety and health initiatives for one of the country's largest turnkey engineering, construction, maintenance, and fabrication services firms.

By role:

The information, processes, and tools outlined in Recipe for Business Success are immediately relevant for middle, senior, and executive management. Recipe for Business Success could also be a beneficial component of professional development programs for aspiring talent, and undergraduate or graduate business school curriculum.

The narrative to follow includes 3 Parts, each dedicated to one 'ingredient' in our Recipe for Business Success. Each "Part" includes an introduction, 3 chapters focused on developing the 'ingredient' and outlining 'how to' steps to the recipe, and a summary chapter that includes appropriate portions of the ASCEND story, top takeaways and tips on implementation, and citations and references. It will be helpful to have a high-level understanding of what will follow so that topics can be put into context as we explore each ingredient.

Part I - Culture

Chapter 1 introduces the concept of culture, the values, systems, attitudes, and set of assumptions that people in an organization share and adopt to achieve stated goals and objectives. In chapter 2, we describe 3 elements to an organization's core ideology, including:

- Core Purpose – describing *Why we exist*; our *noble cause*
- Cultural Beliefs and Values - describing *How we behave*
- Mission - describing *What we do*

In chapter 3 we explore techniques to assess each of these attributes as they exist today and create a vision of where the culture might aspire. This includes a 5-step process to define Core Purpose, using culture walks, interviews, and surveys to uncover Cultural Beliefs, and a 10-step process to uncover (core and aspirational) Values. An exercise for creating a compelling Mission statement that describes "What we do" and reflects why customers chose to spend their time or money with you is also outlined.

Chapter 4 establishes the importance of alignment of culture with strategy, and explores how to progress from where an organization's culture is today to the desired, aspirational culture of the future. It includes a 7-step process to implement and maintain the desired culture, built upon a framework of human behavior and neuropsychology that underpins cultural change.

The key elements of Part I on Culture are summarized in chapter 5. It includes the portion of the ASCEND Summit LLC journey to define and implement their desired culture. The author's suggested Top 10 Takeaways are provided to focus attention on key issues. And the Top 10 Tips for Implementing Part I highlight key considerations necessary to add the Culture ingredient to an organization's unique Recipe for Business Success. Detailed citations and references, along with additional sources of relevant information are also provided.

Part II - Strategy

Chapter 6 introduces strategy; the art and science of deploying resources to achieve stated goals of an organization at an enterprise, business unit, or product or service line level. Strategy describes in broad terms how goals are to be achieved and marshals the resources (people, time, money) for their most efficient and effective use. Strategy requires a well-developed roadmap for getting to the desired destination, and in the Recipe for Business Success, this roadmap is the outcome of a strategic planning process.

Chapter 7 offers an exacting definition of strategic planning and provides insights on advantages and disadvantages of varying forms of this essential business process. Chapter 8 explores in detail each element of a comprehensive, flexible planning model.

Suggested techniques and tools for implementing an effective strategic planning process are outlined in chapter 9. This includes consideration of selection of participants for a strategic planning workshop, and engaging a board of directors or other leadership in a 5-step Strategic Envisioning exercise. It includes suggested exercises for conducting SWOT analysis of information on the present state health of an organization, development of a Vision statement and Overarching Goals, and a Plan for Success or roadmap for moving from the present state to the desired future state.

As outlined above in Part I, the key elements of Part II on Strategy (applicable portions of the ASCEND story, top takeaways, top implementation tips, and citations and references) are summarized in chapter 10.

Part III - Execution

Chapter 11 introduces the concept of Execution as involving having the right people required to support the organization's strategy and making sure they are efficiently doing what is needed to achieve the most important strategic goals. In chapter 12 we explore 3 prerequisites to efficient and effective Execution. It provides a how-to guide for 1) establishing a positive culture of accountability, 2) aligning leadership practices with the intended strategy and culture, and 3) embracing lifelong learning to remain agile and open-minded during an era of exponential rate of change.

In chapter 13 we explore two key areas to effectively implementing and maintaining organizational culture. Chapter 13 describes the use of cultural assessments and cultural interviewing techniques during the recruiting and selection of new talent, and use of an employee-driven performance management process to develop existing talent, including essential managerial coaching techniques.

Similarly, in chapter 14, we explore the keys to executing on strategy, including an implementation timeline to ensure strategic planning remains an ongoing process through establishing initial long-range goals, annual objective setting, and quarterly Review

& Reload sessions to monitor progress and make necessary course corrections.

As in the previous parts, the key elements of Part III on Execution (applicable portions of the ASCEND story, top takeaways, top implementation tips, and citations and references) are summarized in chapter 15.

In summary, each Part...

- Includes an *introduction* to set the stage,
- Creates a functional definition of the ingredient,
- Establishes "why" it is essential to achieving Success,
- Describes processes and tools to add the ingredient to the mix,
- Provides an illustration of the process through description of the ASCEND story, and
- Summarizes top takeaways, top implementation tips, citations and references.

Recipe for Business Success only has three essential ingredients, but there are a range of issues to consider when adding culture, strategy, and execution to the mix. The Epilogue captures these concerns.

Epilogue

In the Epilogue, we describe steps necessary to ensure that Culture, Strategy, and Execution are not seen as independent variables, but where each has a role to play in and are essential ingredients to our Recipe for Business Success. The Epilogue reinforces the notion that this is not a "one size fits all" approach. To the contrary, the chef for this recipe is encouraged to exercise discretion and customize each element of the recipe to align with the unique needs of their organization.

Appendices

Describing the process followed by a small but growing business in the personal fitness space at the conclusion of each Part helps readers visualize how the recipe can be applied to their organizations. To help readers further, a copy of the resulting plan for ASCEND Summit LLC is included as Appendix 1.

There are many steps involved with the addition of each ingredient to our Recipe for Business Success. Select tools are imbedded within the corresponding text to help illustrate a step. Additional tools are provided in Appendix 2, including a form to support collection and analysis of responses during the Strategic Envisioning exercise (described in chapter 9), and a template document for capturing your unique culture and outlining your unique strategic plan resulting from Parts I and II.

Various jargon is used throughout Recipe for Business Success. Many words and phrases are terms of art that have specific meaning when used in the particular context of our recipe but might have a different meaning in common use. Appendix 3, Definitions – *The Language of Business Success*, consolidates and defines key jargon as used and cited throughout the text.

As might be expected, there is no shortage of proposed methods and models available to address each of the 3 ingredients for Success. No attempt is made to create an exhaustive inventory, let alone an assessment of these methodologies. Instead, the models, tools, and processes included herein should be viewed as illustrative. This book is designed to be both thought provoking and how-to cookbook. It provides background information on each 'ingredient' and a practical Recipe for Business Success. When possible, examples are provided to illustrate how each 'ingredient' might be added to each organization's unique Recipe for Business Success. But this is no precise cookbook, as none of this is 'one size fits all.' Just as a chef at a small restaurant must develop the menu and serve the customer along with preparing the meals, organizational leaders will need to adopt the models, tools, and processes in manners that are best suited to their particular circumstances. The methods or processes described can and should be modified to meet the intended purpose within a given organization.

Citations and References

1. Mercer, LLC, *The Purpose of Corporations: A Tale of Two Theories*, February 2020, https://www.marshmclennan. com/content/dam/mmc-web/insights/publications/2020/ february/gl-2020-the-purpose-of-corporations-a-tale-of-two-theories.pdf.
2. Martin Lipton, "The Friedman Essay and the True Purpose of the Business Corporation," Harvard Law School Forum on Corporate Governance, September 17, 2020, https://corpgov.law.harvard.edu/2020/09/17/ the-friedman-essay-and-the-true-purpose-of-the-business-corporation/.

Part I
CULTURE

Chapter 1

AN INTRODUCTION TO CULTURE

E very company has a culture. It is composed of the values, systems, attitudes, and set of assumptions that people in an organization share and adopt to achieve stated goals and objectives. These attributes are definable by observing how people work together and interact in carrying out the mission of the company.

Some companies give little attention to culture and simply allow things to happen. Others study the culture they have, create a picture of where they want to be, and implement a strategy to establish and maintain a desired culture. Regardless of which end of this spectrum an organization is on, they have the culture they deserve. That is, organizational culture is a choice.

When tasked to create a list as long as necessary but as short as possible to describe what it takes to be successful in business, we suggested in the prologue that most responses would fall within three barrels. Along with having a well-defined strategy and the ability to execute on that plan, most would agree that culture, and specifically the people that make up that culture, are essential parts of business success. Perhaps that is the sentiment reflected in the oft-cited maxim "Our people are our most important asset." Some place exceptional importance on culture. You may have heard the famous quote variously attributed that "culture eats strategy for breakfast." This shouldn't be taken to mean that strategy is unimportant—rather a more informed perspective is that a powerful and empowering culture creates a promising route to organizational success.

> **For the greatest opportunity for success, business strategy must be built upon an organization's culture, and organizational culture must be aligned with and supportive of the business strategy.**

The problem with a literal interpretation of the expression is that it separates culture from strategy and execution, as if they were independent variables where you could have one without the other. Alternatively, it places culture on higher ground, suggesting that it is far more important than strategy. As the diagram infers, Culture, Strategy, and disciplined Execution of plans each have essential roles to play in achieving Success. The expression "culture constrains strategy," also variously attributed, better reflects business realities. Without an adequate, aligned, and supportive culture, developing and implementing strategy will surely be constrained. Our belief is that success is far more likely to occur when a relevant plan (Strategy) is aggressively implemented (Execution) by an aligned and fully engaged workforce (Culture).

Figure 1.1: Recipe for business success

While disagreeing with the underlying premise that culture trumps strategy, a legitimate question arises – just how do they relate? Daniel Patrick Forrester, Founder and Board Chair of Thruue, a culture and strategy consultancy, concluded in an article titled *Culture, Strategy and Harvard Business Review* that culture cannot easily be divorced from strategy. "Strategy is the front wheel and handlebars of the bike, and culture is the chain, cogs, and back wheel. Leaders will win the race only when they allow the two halves to work together."[1] The metaphor is illustrated in the figure below.

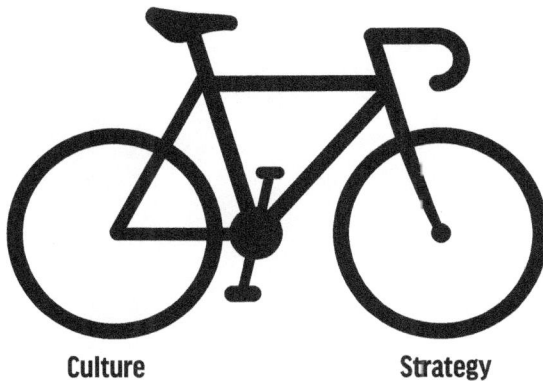

Culture   Strategy

Figure 1.2: Two parts of an integrated system

With this view, culture and strategy are two parts of an integrated system. In practice, they must work together, in unison and harmony to achieve the best outcomes. For the greatest opportunity for success, business strategy must be built upon an organization's culture, and organizational culture must be aligned with and supportive of the business strategy.

The premise for this ingredient in our Recipe for Business Success is simple: Culture is at the heart of a company. If we want to have successful organizations that are sustainable over time, setting and maintaining culture must be an ongoing, intentional initiative. For this reason, we will introduce Culture as the first ingredient in our Recipe for Business Success. Chapter 2 describes the elements of an organization's Core Ideology that collectively capture the culture ingredient in our Recipe for Business Success. Chapter 3 outlines steps that might be followed to define and characterize existing and desired culture, while chapter 4 describes considerations and approaches for moving towards the desired destination.

Chapter 2

ELEMENTS OF CORE IDEOLOGY

" **I**deology" has been described as a systematic body of concepts or characteristics of an individual, group, or culture. Others describe ideology as a body of beliefs that guide individuals or large groups. The subtle distinction is that the first definition infers a passive observation of existing ideology, while the second suggests using ideology as guidance. Both descriptions are accurate and meaningful; we want to be able to observe and describe our ideology **and** use it to guide our strategy for success. For the purposes of our discussions, Core Ideology is built upon three elements, as illustrated below:

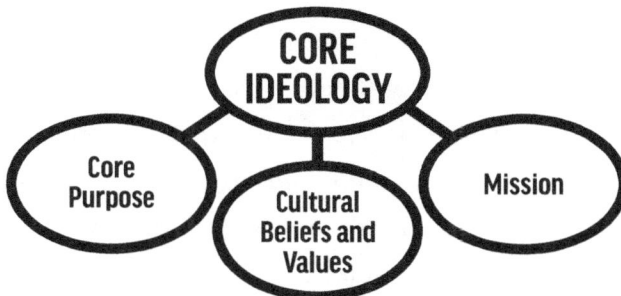

Figure 2.1: The Core Ideology triad

Core Ideology includes statements of:

- Core Purpose – describing **Why** we exist; our *noble cause*
- Cultural Beliefs and Values – describing **How** we behave
- Mission – describing **What** we do

Core Purpose

In 2009, Simon Sinek, author of *Leaders Eat Last* and *Together is Better*, started what has been characterized as a movement with release of his book *Start with Why: How Great Leaders Inspire Everyone to Take Action*. Since then, millions have watched his TED Talk based on the *Start with Why* premise.

In both the book and TED Talk, Sinek starts with a fundamental question: Why are some people and organizations more innovative, more influential, and more profitable than others? He suggests that people like Martin Luther King Jr., Steve Jobs, and the Wright Brothers had little in common, but they all started with Why. They realized that people won't truly buy into a product, service, movement, or idea until they understand the Why behind it.[2] This has become especially important in employee recruitment, avoiding 'quiet quitting,' and retention of engaged talent. People are looking beyond 'just a paycheck' and seeking purpose in their work. And it extends to customers as well. Customers want to know your story. People want to buy from and work with people they like, understand, and share common values. Your story – not just what you do and how you do it, but **why** you do it – helps create that emotional connection that is critical to long-term relationships and sustainability. Consider those lucky few that find an auto repair shop whose 'why' embraces building trust-based relationships. Customers will likely return on a repeat basis because they feel confident in their decision to use these services and appreciate the honesty of the staff.

The process of developing a statement of Core Purpose that describes *Why we exist; our noble cause* will be discussed in chapter 3. For now, it is important to recognize that answering the question of Core Purpose is **the** foundational element of culture and part of the triad of Core Ideology.

Cultural Beliefs and Values

Cultural Beliefs and Values play an integral part in the Core Ideology triad and ultimately play the biggest role in defining the Culture ingredient in our Recipe for Business Success. To engage in strategic thinking and execute those plans, one must have a deep appreciation for how people are expected to behave.

Cultural Beliefs

Cultural beliefs describe how people individually and collectively interact with one another to accomplish tasks. If organizational psychologists were to visit your company offices, field sites, and production floors, how would they describe how people work together to get things done? If they sat in on your meetings, or listened in on calls or studied your correspondence with each other and your customers, how would they describe those interactions? These observations describe the organization's cultural norms. Often, cultural beliefs are implied, not expressly defined, and develop organically over time from the cumulative traits of the people the organization hires and retains. Rather than leave standards for acceptable behavior to chance and at everyone's discretion, our Recipe for Business Success anticipates intentionally establishing a code of acceptable, expected behaviors that are supportive of and in alignment with the organization's strategy.

What is most conducive to success is that culture be shared throughout the organization, and intentionally designed to be aligned with and supportive of the organization's mission and vision.

Every organization (i.e., enterprise, business unit, or product/service line team) has its own culture. There aren't necessarily "right" or "wrong" cultures — it mainly depends on what is important to the organization. What is most conducive to success is that culture be shared throughout the organization, and intentionally designed to be aligned with and supportive of the organization's mission and vision. Simple words like respectful, innovative, or honest help describe beliefs and values but do not adequately define culture. The range of workplace characteristics explored in cultural assessments include attributes like those listed in the table below, which have been adopted from The Culture Keys in Edgar Papke's *True Alignment: Linking Company Culture with Customer Needs for Extraordinary Results*[3]:

Table 2.1 – Illustrative list of cultural attributes

How do people individually and collectively interact...

Conflict Resolution – systematic or ad hoc; centered on people or process

Customer Engagement – degree of urgency; speed of reaction vs. quality of response

Decision Making – Flexible vs. controlled; individual, team or group; level of authority

Organizational structure – Hierarchical, horizontal, functional, divisional, matrix, team-based, network, or some combination thereof; focused internally or externally

Planning & Goal Setting – Collaborative, cascaded, or authoritarian

Power & Influence – concentrated vs dispersed

Problem Solving – centered on process or people; individual or team; level of trust

Recognition & Rewards – based upon desired outcome or level of effort; types of equity

Talent management – role of cultural alignment in hiring, promotions, compensation

Teamwork – organized around expertise, cross-functional generalist, or personal interest

There are three broad approaches to assessing these and other cultural beliefs of an organization. They include culture walks, culture interviews, and culture surveys. Collectively, these three cultural assessment techniques involve impartial observation and reporting on observable behaviors and reported beliefs of (all levels of) employees. These methodologies will be described more fully in chapter 3.

Values

Values are an important component of organizational culture. There are many values that individuals or organizations may embrace, but core values rise to the top. They represent the highest priorities of existing, deeply held beliefs. Aspirational values are those that a company needs to succeed in the future but currently lacks or are not fully realized. Jim Collins, author of *Good to Great*, offered practical insights on the distinction between **core values** and **aspirational values:**

> *People frequently confuse timeless core values—what you truly believe and have always believed at a deep core level—with aspirations of what you'd like to see the organization become in the future. You may have such an aspiration, but if you are honest with yourself and it is not a core value for the people in your breakout group, the place to put it is in the vivid description aspect of the Envisioned Future. Do not mix future aspirations into your true and authentic core values, as this will create justifiable cynicism and destroy the power of your core values. For example, a group that has never held innovation as a core value should not put innovation into its list of core values, even if it sees innovation as a vital strategy for its future. Instead, it should make innovation part of its Envisioned Future a quality that it wants to stimulate progress toward.*[4]

Combined, core and aspirational values define what the organization stands for in the world and provide the litmus test against which all actions and behaviors should be measured. These values also help companies determine if they are on the right path and fulfill their goals by creating an unwavering guide.

Values help define which strategies an organization pursues to fulfill its mission, underlie all their work, and along with cultural beliefs, define how to interact with each other. Like core purpose, they are fundamental to attracting and retaining the 'right' talent, and an important part of the story customers want to know to do business with you. A simple technique will be presented in chapter 3 to help an organization identify those core and aspirational values which form the foundation on which Strategy is developed and work is Executed.

Mission

In our triad model of Core Ideology, a Mission statement is designed to describe *What we do*. Mission statements of organizations are, theoretically, built upon its Core Purpose, and Cultural Beliefs and Values, and act as a reality-check when new products or services are launched. Based upon a compilation of sources and experiences, a well written Mission statement should:

- Describe how an organization fulfills its Core Purpose and Vision
- Be externally oriented yet inspire people within the organization to do their personal best
- Convey the human emotion and motivation of employees and customers that buy into '*What we do*'

Some suggest a mission statement describes the "what," the "who," and the "why," of a company. Others rattle off the trio of mission, vision, and values as if they are one catchy phrase when, in fact, they are three very distinct concepts for organizations. The line gets especially blurred with mission and vision statements.

The distinction is quite simple. A mission statement focuses on today and describes *What we do*. The vision statement (described more fully in Part II on Strategy) focuses on tomorrow and describes *What we want to become*. While some organizations continue to (mis)use mission and vision statements interchangeably, it's important to have both. They are distinct, serve differing purposes, and one doesn't work without the other. Developing a mission statement will be addressed in chapter 3.

Summary

Core ideology systematically describes the body of characteristics of an organization's culture. Core ideology describes the beliefs that guide all aspects of the organization. Core ideology is built upon three elements as listed below:

- Core Purpose – describing **Why** *we exist;* our *noble cause*
- Cultural Beliefs and Values - describing **How** *we behave*
- Mission - describing **What** *we do*

As illustrated below, Core Ideology is simultaneously hierarchical – with Core Purpose perched at the top – and circular, as *Why we exist* informs *How we behave*, which enables *What it is we do*, which reinforces *Why we exist*, and so on.

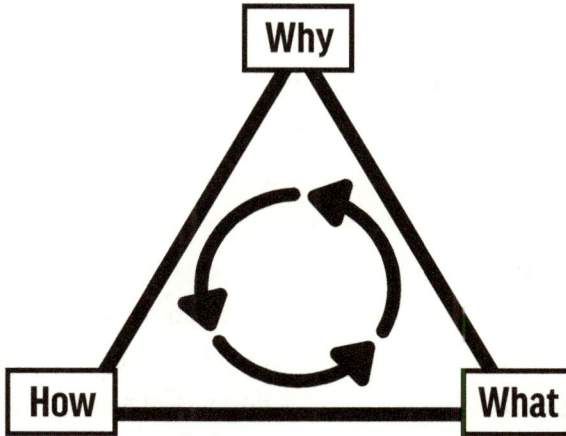

Figure 2.2: The Core Ideology interplay

In chapter 3 we will explore techniques for defining each of these distinct but complimentary elements of an organization's core ideology. In chapter 4 we will explore the steps required to implement and maintain a desired culture. Like everything in this book, this Recipe emerged from knowledge and experience gained throughout my professional career, and specifically while serving as CEO during the final ten years of my 25-plus year career with KTA-Tator, Inc. (KTA). See the boxout for additional background on KTA and the genesis of our cultural journey.

OUR CULTURE JOURNEY AT KTA

KTA has a storied history of customer-driven innovation. Kenneth Tator was finishing work for the Pentagon War Production Board during World War II when he embarked on a career in the corrosion protection industry. He launched Kenneth Tator Associates from his home in 1949, with the invention of a composite test panel to conduct comparative testing of industrial paint systems from different manufacturers. Clients soon engaged Mr. Tator as a consultant to determine why existing systems were failing, and to develop specifications to properly install the correct coating systems as determined by the outcomes of his comparative studies.

As testing and consulting work expanded, Mr. Tator saw the opportunity to respond to an emerging need for inspection services to verify fieldwork was performed in accordance with good painting practices and the specifications he had written. Ken Tator took over from his father in 1969. Shortly thereafter Ken saw the opportunity for KTA to provide these 3rd-party coatings inspection to the emerging nuclear energy industry. During the 'heyday' of service to the nuclear industry, Ken invested heavily in expanding KTA's physical testing and analytical services to create the first full-service 3rd-party coatings laboratory operation in the country. And when Congress first authorized the use of federal funds for highway maintenance in 1991, KTA was poised to shift its attention to the emerging bridge maintenance and rehabilitation market.

KTA recognized the need for a combination of steel fabrication inspection and coatings inspection during the manufacture of new steel bridges and responded by hiring Certified Welding Inspectors and training them in coatings inspection. By 1999, a separate business unit was created that would later add concrete fabrication inspection and Non-Destructive Examination to its portfolio of structural materials integrity testing services. KTA also added significant corrosion engineering and cathodic protection talent through the acquisition of Elzly Technology Corporation.

These milestone events and associated growth in the depth and breadth of services allowed KTA to become 100-percent employee owned through an Employee Stock Ownership Plan, or ESOP. Throughout his ownership, Ken Tator had embraced an entrepreneurial management style and a family-values-oriented culture. The change in ownership created the opportunity, if not the need, to design the ideal culture for moving our employee-owned company into the future.

Our journey started with the leadership team challenging the core purpose statement I had drafted and further vetting it with a select group of co-owners over a 3-month period. The leadership team undertook a year-long study of culture through the review and discussion of selected books and articles. Formal and informal cultural assessments were completed, ultimately resulting in the codification of our cultural beliefs. We didn't have a name for it at the time, but we assembled a group of key influencers from across the organization to help identify and define our values. This same group of influencers participated in strategic planning exercises, which included (re)defining our mission.

The entire process took over a year. Much of this work was intuitive. It was only in hindsight that the cultural elements and processes in this Recipe for Business Success emerged. The resultant core ideology is now embraced by new leadership as their nation-wide materials engineering, inspection, and testing company continues to pursue its mission of protecting clients' assets and the world's infrastructure.

Chapter 3

DEFINING CORE IDEOLOGY

The first step in developing the triad that makes up Core Ideology is perhaps the most important step as it underlies the "Why" for the organization. Developing any form of meaningful statement about an organization (e.g., mission, vision) is challenging when done by committee. In the case of core purpose, a top-down approach is suggested, as establishing one's "noble cause" should have notional direction from the top.

Core Purpose

Developing a Core Purpose Statement (CPS) that describes *Why we exist* should be an iterative process that starts with the top executive, expands to a trusted team of executive leadership, and is ultimately beta-tested within a larger community of stakeholders. All involved should know that a CPS is not a mission statement that describes *What we do* or a vision statement that describes *What we want to become*. The CPS answers a more fundamental question of *Why do we exist?* Or put differently, *What is our noble cause?* As the name infers, a CPS gives all stakeholders a sense of purpose.

Establishing a Core Purpose Statement

There are numerous suggested methodologies for developing effective core purpose statements accessible with a simple internet search using the subject heading above. Links to a few example sites are listed in the citations in chapter 5.[5,6] The four-step process outlined below is drawn from multiple sources and personal experience. It is not a rigid protocol but more of a framework for the creative work necessary to develop an effective Core Purpose Statement:

1. CEO's Introspection

The first step in the process involves inner reflection on the past, present, and future of the organization.

- *Reflecting on the past.* What was the driving force for creating the organization? Was it connected to a passion; area of expertise; a particular technology, product, or service; an emotional drive to create a new path/breakthrough; or something more basic like making money?
- *Assessing the present.* Since the start, what's changed about the organization, and what's remained constant? Why are the organization's products or services beneficial to customers? What problems do they solve? How does the organization identify and address customer needs? What makes the company unique in the marketplace? And the most challenging question: With all the options in the marketplace, why do customers choose to spend their time or money with your organization?

One method to address the present is to start with *What you do*. Write the statement on a flip chart or white board: "We make X products or deliver Y services." Next, ask "Why is that important"? Write the answer on the flip chart or whiteboard. Ask the Why question again and again (up to five times), each time brainstorming and charting your answers.

- *Contemplating the future.* What inspires and motivates you about the future?

2. Create a draft

Distill what you've written down in answer to the questions outlined above into five or so alternative sentences of a few words that fit on a single line and describe why you exist; your noble cause:

Identify any key words that appear in all or several of the single sentences above (i.e., words or concepts that appear multiple times). Distill the list down to 5 or 6 key words.

Think about these key words and incorporate (all of) them into an initial draft CPS. In drafting the initial statement, it should be understood that unlike a goal or objective, you cannot fulfill a purpose; it is like a guiding star on the horizon – forever pursued but never reached.

```

```

Some examples may be helpful:

- **3M:** To solve unsolved problems innovatively
- **Mary Kay Cosmetics:** To give unlimited opportunity to women
- **Merck:** To preserve and improve human life
- **NIKE:** To bring inspiration and innovation to every athlete in the world
- **Patagonia:** To be a role model and tool for social change
- **Telecare:** To help people with mental impairments realize their full potential
- **Walt Disney:** To make people happy

3. Get Feedback - Does the Core Purpose align with your values?

It is important to seek out feedback from others after you develop your initial draft. Start with the executive or senior leadership team. They need to buy into the CPS as much as anyone as they will ultimately be tasked with embracing it. Describe the introspective steps you have taken, the draft statements and resultant identification of key words, and your initial draft statement. Let them process this for a quarter or two to determine if you have it right. Does it resonate with why they come to work every day? Is the draft CPS:

- Aspirational, like a guiding star on the horizon – forever pursued but never reached?
- Open ended – will it fit as products or services offered change?
- Abstract enough to be inspiring, but also descriptive enough to work toward it?

As a final step, it is important to ask for feedback from a larger stakeholder (e.g., board of directors, shareholders, members, etc.) and employee audience. Explain the questions behind a CPS – *Why do we exist? What is our noble cause?* Encourage those you reach out to share their insights and opinions.

4. Finalize the Core Purpose statement

After soliciting and considering all the feedback, create a final draft, but do not distribute it until after the next step in defining Core Ideology is complete. That is, the final Core Purpose must be in alignment with Cultural Beliefs and Values, and visa-versa.

Following the process described above culminated with the following Core Purpose statement for KTA-Tator, Inc. (KTA), the 100-percent employee-owned S-Corp ESOP materials engineering, inspection, and testing firm introduced at the end of chapter 2:

Building meaningful careers,
worthwhile businesses, fulfilling lives

KTA's final Core Purpose was introduced to all co-owners in part via multi-fold pamphlet, the inside cover of which is illustrated below:

As indicated previously, additional resources for developing core purpose statements are listed in the Citations and References for Part I found at the end of chapter 5.

Cultural Beliefs and Values

The next step in the process of defining Core Ideology is designed to answer the question *How do we behave?* The answer lies in the cultural beliefs and values expressed and embraced throughout the organization. The following narrative outlines a collaborative approach to characterizing these fundamental attributes.

Cultural Beliefs

Cultural assessments are used to uncover and describe deeply rooted beliefs that are the drivers of people's behavior and accepted norms. Cultural assessments help organizations describe their true organizational culture (i.e., the present state), define their ideal culture (i.e., the destination) and characterize the difference between them.

As introduced in chapter 2 and more fully described in an article *How to Understand Your Current Company Culture* by the team at LiveAbout,[7] it is generally recognized that there are three broad approaches to cultural assessments of an organization. They include:

- Culture walks – designed to impartially observe organizational culture in action
- Culture interviews – designed to hear what small groups of employees say about culture and observe the behaviors and interactions of participant during these conversations
- Culture surveys – designed around written or online instruments using questions designed to gain insights on culture from a representative cross-section or all employees

All three techniques involve impartial observation and reporting on observable behaviors and reported beliefs of (all levels of) employees designed to evaluate and differentiate between an ideal culture and an organization's actual or true culture. Decisions may be made to employ any one of the techniques, a combination thereof, or hybrid specifically designed to meet the anticipated needs of the organization (i.e., enterprise, business unit, or product/service line team).

Conducting these evaluations includes assessing various components of culture, such as those examples listed in the sidebar (which were more fully described in Table 2.1). Note that the list is illustrative and not considered exhaustive. The evaluations can be self-performed, conducted by professional consultants, use commercially available assessment tools, or some combination thereof. Note, however, that it is difficult to assess your own culture without introducing bias or raising suspicions regarding your motives by those being observed. A conscious and intentional effort must be made to fully explain the intended purpose and subsequently become an impartial observer of your culture in action; to observe, document, and report on what is present, and what is not there, without interference.

CULTURAL ATTRIBUTES
Conflict Resolution
Customer Engagement
Decision Making
Organizational structure
Planning & Goal Setting
Power & Influence
Problem Solving
Recognition & Rewards
Talent management
Teamwork

Culture Walks

As described above, culture walks are used to impartially observe organizational culture in action. Cultural assessments require objective observations about the physical workspace and appurtenance, the interactions of workers, the conduct of meetings, and behaviors of teams. By their very nature, culture walks are less data-driven components of cultural assessments, aimed at assessing tangible aspects of culture like the design of workspaces, and intangible aspects of culture like level of energy or sense of urgency. While the observer may wish to develop a list of questions to be answered using the listing of cultural attributes in Table 2.1 or examples in the referenced article from LiveAbout[7], the true challenge is to simply observe, document, and report on actual objective observations of what is present (e.g., worker/supervisor interactions) or absent (e.g., teamwork). In drawing conclusions, what do the impartial, unobtrusive observations say about how people work together to get things done? What do they say about interactions in meetings, or on calls, or in written correspondence with each other and customers?

Culture Interviews

As described above, culture interviews are designed to hear what small groups of employees say about culture while simultaneously observing the behaviors and interactions of participants during these conversations. The goal is to solicit feedback about workplace behaviors and patterns they (employees) have observed (as opposed to those of an observer during a culture walk). Many of the questions asked during interviews with small groups may be the same, or similar, to those used in a culture survey (described below). The challenge is to listen and acknowledge, but not respond to the observations offered by the participants.

Asking (some of) the same questions in small group meetings and in a survey may reveal important insights about employees' sense of trust if the answers are widely different. Areas that can be effectively explored during culture interviews include questions about organizational agility or adaptability, individual level of empowerment/authority to make decisions, management support and direction, management recognition of employee concerns, and level of employee engagement. In drawing conclusions, what do the participants say about how people feel about the organization, executive and senior leadership, immediate supervisors and managers, peers and team members, and themselves? How do they feel about the mission and vision of the organization, leadership's priorities, and company beliefs and values? What do the interactions during the culture interview meetings reveal?

Culture Surveys - general

Culture surveys involve written or online instruments using questions designed to gain insights on culture from all or a representative cross-section of employees. Culture surveys are particularly challenging for small businesses that want to design and administer self-assessments. There is an art and science involved in the development of valid individual survey questions and associated response options. The range of questions asked must address the desired universe of cultural attributes (see Table 2.1 and LiveAbout post[7] for examples). The mechanism to collect and compile responses, and then translate the results into actionable items and/or measurable indicators of performance (for subsequent reevaluation), must all be factored into the original design before initiating the survey. While described below, the resources required (people, time, money) to completely design and administer custom-designed cultural surveys may not warrant the expense.

Culture surveys – custom designed

It is wise to conduct adequate research on survey-design if a decision is made to design and administer an internally developed culture survey. It is important to create the survey using insights gained from culture walks and culture interviews. The minimum steps involved should include:

1. Identify the cultural attributes to be considered (e.g., see Table 2.1).
2. Develop a set of questions to explicitly explore each attribute based upon insights gained during culture walks and culture interviews. Consider if survey responses will be simple true/false, multiple choice, gradient (e.g., 1-5 from Strongly Disagree to Strongly Agree), or open-ended.

3. Ensure the survey responses can be compiled and analyzed in a meaningful way that will actually help characterize the existing and desired culture.

As previously introduced, Edgar Papke, author of *True Alignment – Linking Company Culture with Customer Needs for Extraordinary Results*, describes 12 Culture Keys that define the underlying emotional forces that influence workplace behaviors. Areas to explore to assess these Culture Keys are described in the referenced text. Review of books like *True Alignment*, articles in professional journals, or the content (blogs) on the websites of online vendors like those described below, will prove valuable when custom designing a culture survey.

Having said all of this, I'd like to repeat: the resources required (people, time, money) to completely design and administer custom-designed cultural surveys may not warrant the expense. Use of commercially available surveys as described below may be preferable.

Cultural surveys – online instruments

Rather than a custom-designed survey, consideration should be given to 'off-the-shelf' surveys, even though they may have questions that are not relevant to your organization. In addition, if the survey instrument has been used in several other organizations, the questions may be more reliable and validated. There are numerous online survey instruments available for consideration.

The Organizational Culture Assessment Instrument (OCAI)©, developed by Kim Cameron and Robert Quinn at the University of Michigan, is offered as a validated research method to assess organizational culture. Multiple practitioners utilize the OCAI model in their work, such as:

- QuestionPro https://www.questionpro.com/
- OCAIonline https://www.ocai-online.com/

Other vendors rely on multiple tools including their own proprietary surveys, such as:

- SurveyAnyplace https://surveyanyplace.com/use-cases/culture-assessment/
- TestGorilla https://www.testgorilla.com/

Another source of cultural assessment support could be industry or professional associations. For instance, the National Center for Employee Ownership's (NCEO) *Ownership Culture Survey* provides the tools to measure culture effectively in ESOP-owned companies. Survey results include a comparison of data from over 18,000 respondents at more than 100 companies. Such benchmarking among peer groups could be a value-added component of a culture survey.

In summary, as more fully described by the editorial team at Indeed,[8] the steps involved to fully characterize existing cultural beliefs include:

1. Select a cultural assessment model – involving culture walks, culture interviews, culture surveys, a combination thereof, or a hybrid approach necessary to gain the desired perspective.
2. Conduct the assessment (i.e., culture walk, interview, and/or survey) impartially – limiting observer and survey bias.
3. Objectively compile and analyze results – identifying patterns of observations and responses, and relating them to specific cultural attributes.

4. Draw conclusions – create a verbal picture of the existing culture as it would be described by an impartial observer.

Once the existing cultural beliefs are understood and defined, a strategy can be developed to create desired cultural changes. This will be explored further in chapter 4. For now, it is important to emphasize that company culture will evolve and change, either with intent or simply as the workforce changes due to voluntary or involuntary turnover, growth of the organization, etc. Therefore, the form of cultural assessment selected should consider the need to track progress and/or repeat the process at some later date and compare outcomes in a meaningful way.

Following a hybrid version of the processes described above culminated with the following example statement of Cultural Beliefs for KTA, which was introduced to all co-owners as part of the multi-fold pamphlet, which is illustrated below:

CULTURAL BELIEFS

OUR CULTURE Provides a competitive advantage through an environment where we demonstrate:

Participation
in developing strategy - we expect and encourage employee engagement.

Expertise
in execution of our strategy and delivery of our promise to the customer - we rely on strong subject matter expertise.

Authenticity
in dealing with people, driven by our core values and beliefs.

Workshopping Values

The other integral component of describing *How we behave* involves characterizing the values of the organization. As described in chapter 2, there are many values that individuals or organizations may embrace, but core values rise to the top. Core values define what the organization stands for in the world and provide the litmus test against which all actions and behaviors can be measured. Core values exist today. As indicated previously, aspirational values are those that a company wants (i.e., to create a desired work environment) or needs (i.e., in support of a new strategy) in the future but currently lacks or are not fully realized.

But how do you identify these highest priorities and deeply held values? While no less important, the process for identifying values can be much more streamlined than the more involved process outlined above for characterizing cultural beliefs.

The first step in identifying values involves selecting participants to be involved in a workshop exercise. Since core values should be reflective of non-negotiable values of the organization, participants should be selected from among a collection of key influencers. Key influencers are people whose opinion and advice are respected and valued by many others within the work environment, irrespective of positional authority, including those working in differing business units and functions.

From within this group of influencers, participants should be selected with a goal of gaining a diverse perspective across the organization. This may involve people from differing business units, hierarchical level, and professional backgrounds or roles. In the end, the participants selected from among the key influencers should reflect a diversity of perspectives on what makes the organization tick. For instance, at KTA we started with a book club team comprised of much of the senior management team and added influencers from targeted areas of operation and differing organizational levels that were underrepresented. On the other hand, as described in The ASCEND Summit, LLC story in chapter 5, I have completed this exercise with as few as the three founders of an entrepreneurial startup operation.

It is desirable to establish two or more teams at the start of the workshop. Work to maintain diversity of perspective within each team while limiting any participants with direct reporting relationships. Directions to the teams are as follows:

Each individual, on their own and with no dialogue among the team, should:

1. Create a list across the top of a page with the names of 3 individuals, past or present, from any aspect of operations, that in their mind best reflect what is most desirable, admirable, and important about the organization. The selected individuals, or "Exemplars," should be excellent models of behavior and represent "All that is good about the organization."
2. Under the name of each Exemplar, list the most important attributes that make them stand out that others might try to emulate.

As a breakout team:

3. Share the list of names of the Exemplars. Write or display them across the top of a whiteboard or screen. If there were 4 people in a breakout team, in theory there could be as many as 12 Exemplars identified. This is seldom the case as individual participants will likely select one or more of the same Exemplars.

4. Add the attributes participants identified under each Exemplars' name. Encourage the team to engage in a conversation about the attributes. Retain those that are shared by the majority, if not all, of the expanded list of Exemplars. In processing this, the team participants may need to reach consensus on what each individual means by the word(s) selected to describe an attribute. For instance, one may use "trustworthy" the same as another uses "integrity."

5. Compile the team's list of Exemplars and the attributes or traits that the team believed as shared by **all** their Exemplars. These are potential core values. Have the team list the attributes or traits shared by most, but not all the Exemplars separately. These are potential aspirational values.

As a group as a whole:

6. Repeat the process described for the team breakout above. The list of Exemplars will be larger, and every participant may not know every Exemplar. Only those of the group that know a given Exemplar should assess whether they demonstrate a given attribute or trait.

7. Those attributes or traits shared by all Exemplars should be compiled. It will likely be a short list. The important attributes or traits shared by the majority, but not all of the Exemplars, should be compiled separately as possible aspirational values.

8. Create an initial definition of what each selected attribute means to the group.

Such an exercise should distill the most important behavioral attributes and traits down to about 4-6 values. Those that the group feels were reflected across **all** the Exemplars are likely already embraced across the broader organization and if so, would be considered core values. Those that the group feels were reflected across the majority, but not all the Exemplars, are possible aspirational values. (Note - The strategic planning process outlined in Part II may also result in the identification of one or more aspirational values the organization needs to fulfill its strategy.)

The work is not done. The values identified by the group must be associated with examples of expected behaviors so that everyone knows what they should expect of others. This is accomplished through the combination of value statements and listing of expected cultural norms.

Value Statements and Cultural Norms

A value statement should be developed for each value. The value statement describes what the value means within the organization. Cultural norms represent examples of specific behaviors that guide the behavior of coworkers. Cultural norms define what is encouraged, discouraged, accepted, or rejected. The section of the Netflix website dedicated to "Jobs" confirms that "We believe a company's actual values are shown by whom they hire, reward or let go. Below are the specific behaviors and skills we care about most. If these values describe you, and the people you want to work with, you're likely to thrive at Netflix." A series of 9 values and associated behaviors follow. Here is one example:

Judgment
- *You make wise decisions despite ambiguity*
- *You use data to inform your intuition and choices*
- *You look beyond symptoms to identify systemic issues*
- *You spend our members' money wisely*

- *You make decisions mostly based on their long term, rather than near term, impact*

Netflix goes on to explain "It's easy to talk about valued behaviors; it's harder to live them. In describing courage we say, *You question colleagues' actions inconsistent with these behaviors.* We all work to keep each other accountable for living up to these standards, especially our leaders." [9]

Following the process outlined above, the group of influencers at KTA identified 4 core values and developed short value statements to describe what each value means. It was introduced to all co-owners as part of the multi-fold pamphlet, as illustrated below:

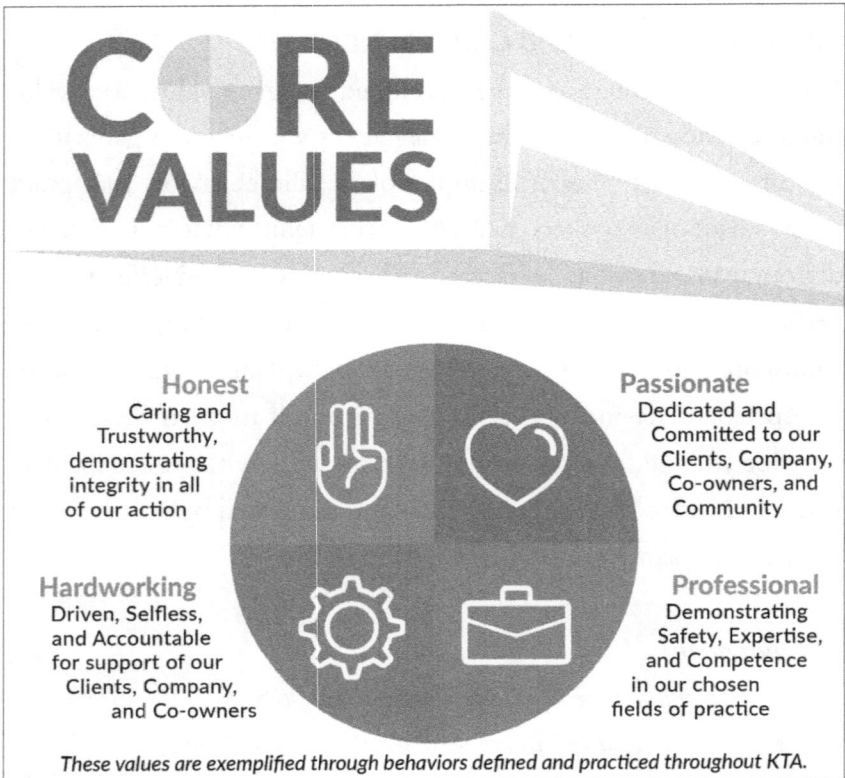

C●RE VALUES

Honest
Caring and Trustworthy, demonstrating integrity in all of our action

Passionate
Dedicated and Committed to our Clients, Company, Co-owners, and Community

Hardworking
Driven, Selfless, and Accountable for support of our Clients, Company, and Co-owners

Professional
Demonstrating Safety, Expertise, and Competence in our chosen fields of practice

These values are exemplified through behaviors defined and practiced throughout KTA.

While not illustrated in the above graphic, the pamphlet also outlined 6-8 cultural norms that describe specific examples of expected behaviors for each of the 4 core values.

One item remains to complete the triad of Core Ideology.

Mission

As described previously in chapter 2, a mission statement is designed to describe *What we do.* A mission statement of an organization should be built upon its Core Purpose, Cultural Beliefs and Values, and not only describe the present but act as catalyst for new products or services. A well written mission statement:

- Describes how an organization fulfills its Core Purpose and Vision
- Is externally oriented yet inspires people within the organization to do their personal best
- Convey the human emotion and motivation of employees and customers that buy into '*What we do*'

The best mission statements support the organization's value proposition. That is, they reflect why customers choose to spend their money with you. The process of developing a mission statement should involve the same or similar participants to the collection of influencers used to develop core and aspirational values described above.

Each team should be asked to generate a list of key attributes that might be addressed within a draft Mission statement. This is not a listing of actual products or services. Instead, it is a listing of attributes that help answer the three prompts listed above. This should involve an exercise in divergent thinking such as asking each participant to call out a possible attribute or characteristic which is recorded without debate or judgement. Characteristics like 'first-in-class,' or 'nation-wide,' or 'sustainable' might be listed. Once an exhaustive list of attributes is developed, the team should use a convergent thinking exercise like placing stickers on their personal top three choices. The team then further reduces the stickered items to identify the top 3-5 attributes they collectively feel are most important to *what we do*.

With these key attributes in mind, each team should prepare an initial draft Mission statement.

All draft statements should be presented and debated as a group. The participants should identify the common attributes from the collection of initial draft statements. Once completed, a 'strawman' Mission statement can be created by the group. It will be subject to review and final editing by executive management but will provide enough notional direction to the question "What is it we do?" Example Mission statements[10] include:

> **Hope Initiative Alliance**: Work together with our partners in improving the quality of life of marginalized people globally.
> **Netflix:** We want to entertain the world.
> **Patagonia:** Build the best product, cause no unnecessary harm, use business to inspire and implement solutions to the environmental crisis.

Southwest Airlines: Connect people to what's most important in their lives through friendly, reliable, and low-cost air travel.
Tesla: Accelerate the world's transition to sustainable energy.
World Kindness Movement: to inspire individuals towards greater kindness and to connect nations to create a kinder world.

As indicated previously, KTA-Tator, Inc. (KTA), is a 100-percent employee-owned S-Corp ESOP materials engineering, inspection, and testing firm. Following the process outlined above, the work of the group of influencers engaged at KTA culminated with the following Vision and Mission statements that were introduced to all co-owners as part of the multi-fold pamphlet, as illustrated below:

INTERNAL **VISION**

We are recognized experts in protecting the world's infrastructure, offering engaged employee-owners both challenges and opportunities throughout their careers, and security during retirement.

EXTERNAL **MISSION**

To provide customer-driven innovation, cutting-edge technology and world-class service delivery for the protection of our customers' assets and the world's infrastructure.

Summary

For the greatest opportunity for success, business strategy must be built upon a company's culture, and company culture must be aligned with and supportive of the business' strategy. In chapter 3 we explored ways to characterize existing and aspirational elements of an organization's Core Ideology. In chapter 4 we will explore how to implement and maintain the Culture ingredient of our Recipe for Business Success, with intent.

Chapter 4

ACHIEVING THE DESIRED CULTURE

The effort required to create meaningful purpose, belief, value, and mission statements is significant. But in a practical sense, the expression of Core Ideology (Core Purpose, Cultural Beliefs and Values, and Mission) resulting from this extensive work can result in little more than a bunch of words. These words need to become a strong guide for how the organization operates in practice. To add the Culture ingredient to your Recipe for Business Success, the desired Core Ideology needs to come alive and be consistently encouraged, recognized, and rewarded across the organization. This chapter focuses on the development of an implementation plan and associated prerequisites to the implementation process. It should be considered in conjunction with Chapter 13: Executing on Culture.

Alignment

As suggested in Chapter 1: Introduction to Culture, culture and strategy are two parts of an integrated system. In practice, they must work together in unison and harmony to achieve the best outcomes. For the greatest opportunity for success, business strategy must be built upon an organization's culture, and organizational culture must be aligned with and supportive of the business strategy.

In chapter 3 we explored ways to characterize the existing culture and paint a picture of the desired Core Ideology for an organization. It included development of statements of:

- Core Purpose – describing *Why we exist;* our *noble cause*
- Cultural Beliefs and Values - describing *How we behave*
- Mission - describing *What we do*

The final step before implementation can begin is ensuring that the desired culture is aligned with and supportive of the business strategy.

In the prologue we suggested that culture represents the shared values, systems, attitudes, and set of assumptions that people in an organization share and adopt to achieve stated goals and objectives. Practitioners like those referenced in chapter 3 use different terminology to describe various types of culture. Depending upon the methodology adopted to complete the cultural assessments (i.e., culture walks, culture interviews, culture surveys, or combination thereof), an overall culture might be defined in singular terms like Innovative, Collaborative, Results Oriented, or Authentic. Regardless of the terminology used, the implied cultural orientation of the term must be aligned with the business strategy the organization intends to engage in to fulfill its mission and strive towards its vision. For example:

- For a manufacturing company that promises to fill all customer orders On Time and In Full (OTIF), a strategically aligned culture would likely embrace tight production targets and distribution deadlines, with an emphasis on winning and outperforming the competition. This strategically aligned culture might be characterized as a **Results-Oriented** or **Compete** culture.

- For a manufacturer promising Zero Defects, a strategically aligned culture would likely embrace a formalized, structured, and bureaucratic workplace, with detailed procedures directing what people do, but empowering workers to take all necessary in-process steps to avoid defects. This strategically aligned culture might be characterized as a **Stable** or **Control** culture.

- For a financial institution that wants to be the locally owned, independent, community bank of choice, a strategically aligned culture would likely embrace a stable and predictable environment with a focus on long-term goals and results, paired with an efficient and smooth execution of tasks. A strategically aligned culture for this organization might also be characterized as a **Stable** or **Control** culture.

- For a startup involved with autonomously operated vehicles, a strategically aligned culture would likely embrace flexibility and adaptability, experimenting with new solutions, and individual initiative and freedom, with little emphasis on hierarchy. This strategically aligned culture might be characterized as a **Creative** or **Innovative** culture.

- For an IT company promoting its open-source platform where their product is completely dependent on people using, sharing, and contributing content, the strategically aligned culture would likely embrace an inclusive community of internal and external stakeholders and brand ambassadors. This strategically aligned culture might be characterized as a **Collaborative** or **Authentic** culture.

- For an institution of higher learning promising transformative experiences, a strategically aligned culture would likely embrace caring for and successfully meeting all aspects of student needs, with an emphasis on preparation for a fulfilling life. This type of culture encourages involvement of all stakeholders in teamwork in the design and maintenance of academic and social traditions. The strategically aligned culture for this organization might be also characterized as a **Collaborative** or **Authentic** culture.

- For charitable associations seeking a world without a specified disease or social ill, a strategically aligned culture would likely embrace stakeholders connecting and working together for the benefit of humanity, conveying a desire to lift the human spirit to achieve their lofty aspirations. Like the IT company and institute of higher learning described above, this strategically aligned culture might also be characterized as a **Collaborative** or **Authentic** culture.

- For a company promoting high-return personal financial planning, a strategically aligned culture would likely embrace figures and numbers being put on the table every time there is a discussion, and managers responsible for success using systems that reward employees based upon their achievements. This strategically aligned culture might be characterized as an **Expertise** or **Results-Oriented** culture.

- For a health care provider promoting holistic patient care, a strategically aligned culture would likely reflect fairness and respecting all individuals involved in patient care. In these organizations, the focus is on caring for others and successfully meeting patient needs, drawing upon the collective expertise of the team. This strategically aligned culture might be characterized as a **Participative** or **Expertise** culture.

- For any type of employee-owned company, regardless of the product or service, a strategically aligned culture would likely embrace fairness and respect for the individual, while promoting teamwork and high-level involvement, resulting in mutual respect. This strategically aligned culture might be characterized as an **Employee-Oriented** or **Participative** culture.

As illustrated in the examples above, organizations don't necessarily need to embrace a singular kind of company culture. In building a strong culture, elements can be pieced together from two or more types with intent to help create the best environment to move the unique organization forward. As the maxim "Culture constrains strategy" suggests, without an aligned and supportive culture, developing and implementing strategy will be stifled. The common attribute of all the examples outlined above is that the business strategy is built upon the organization's culture, and the organization's culture is aligned with and supportive of its business strategy.

Recall that there is no "right" or "wrong" culture. In the end, the Culture component of our Recipe for Business Success requires that the culture of an organization be:

1. Intentionally designed; not left to chance,
2. Supportive of the business strategy, and
3. Embraced across the organization.

Once the desired Core Ideology can be fully described in words (as outlined in chapter 3) and is determined to be in alignment with and supportive of the business strategy (as outlined above), work can begin on ensuring it is embraced across the organization. Some background information on human behavior is necessary before describing steps that might be considered in moving from the existing culture to the desired destination. These are:

- The basics of workforce behavior
- Starting with the destination in mind
- A 7-step framework to moving forward

Basics of Workforce Behavior

As illustrated below, our feelings and beliefs drive our behavior – which in turn causes us to take action and hopefully achieve desired results. The key is that our actions originate based upon our feelings and emotions. There are neuropsychological reasons to support this contention.

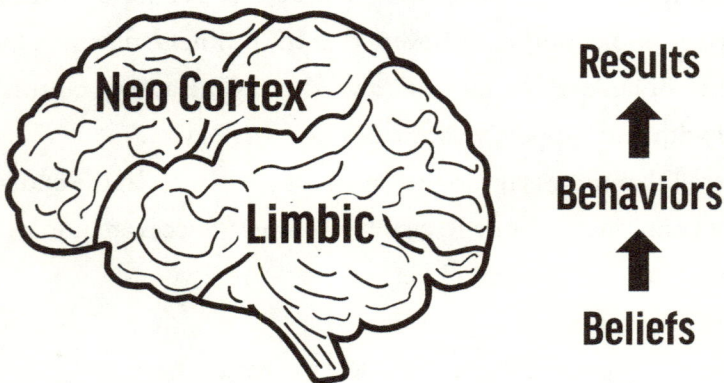

Figure 4.1: Basis for behavioral change

The oldest part of the human brain is the brain stem and limbic system. This is the part of the brain involved in behavioral and emotional responses, especially when it comes to behaviors we need for survival like feeding, reproduction, caring for young, fight or flight, etc.. The neocortex brain is the latest part of human evolution and distinguishes homo sapiens from other species. The neo cortex is the part of the brain where higher cognitive functioning originates. There is no language in the Limbic brain but it is where feelings and emotions exist – where Beliefs are formulated. In humans, our Beliefs (feelings) drive our Behavior (actions), which in turn contribute to the Results (outcomes). [11,12]

Some companies give little attention to culture, and simply allow things to happen, or provide only implicit direction. Others study the culture they have, create a picture of where they want to be, and implement a strategy to establish and maintain a desired culture. Neuroscience suggests that to do so, to change an existing culture, requires influencing peoples' beliefs and the underlying feelings and emotions that support those beliefs.

As a workforce evolves over time, certain norms emerge that describe how people interact, communicate, collaborate, and share. Every workplace has norms; that is, rules and standards that are understood by members of a group, and that guide and/or constrain social behavior. Workplace norms are powerful drivers of human beliefs and behavior.

For example, the sign on the wall and the safety rulebook a new hire signs might implore the adage "Safety First." But if the new hire joins a team that operates equipment without required guards, a group norm emerges. It is reinforced if the team is paid on a daily piecemeal basis, and the supervisor does not act to enforce the safety rules relating to guards. The written rule can say what it may, but the normative (accepted, actual) behavior will likely cause the new hire to believe (feel) 'production is valued more than safety.' The new hire may then behave (act) accordingly, and work without machine guards in place.

Normative behavior typically includes an element of social pressure. An individual's belief about the consequences of a particular behavior is also important. The belief is based on the likelihood that the behavior will produce a given outcome. Observing co-workers engaging in behaviors, such as working without guards in place, may lead an individual to believe the behavior is acceptable. Beyond this, a worker may feel pressure to conform to the normative behavior because a daily incentive is paid based upon team performance. And the belief is reinforced when the supervisor takes no corrective action. However, the reciprocal can also be true. If a new hire observes the team conforming with the written rules and stated values, while promoting teamwork to accomplish production goals, it can reinforce the desired belief that safety and productivity are not mutually exclusive.

Normative beliefs represent an individual's beliefs about the extent to which other (important) people think they should or should not perform particular behaviors. Normative conformity involves changing one's behavior to fit in with the group, regardless of one's personal beliefs. Combined, the normative culture is the body of implicit expectations under which a group of people operate. It puts pressure on individuals to modify their beliefs (feelings), and in turn their behavior (actions), in such a way as to conform to the standards of a group. This means that to change behavior (actions), effort must first be directed at changing worker beliefs (feelings and emotions).

The expression "Easier said than done" seems appropriate, but not if an effective planning model is utilized to create a roadmap.

Start with the Destination in Mind

Regardless of whether a culture is described holistically as Innovative, Collaborative, Results-Oriented, Authentic, or any other label, the critical issue in practice is whether the worker beliefs (feelings) result in the desired behaviors (actions) that are necessary to achieve desired results (outcomes).

The impartial culture walks, culture interviews, and/or culture surveys completed as part of the initial cultural assessment should have established a well-defined picture of the present state of organizational culture (i.e., an inventory of existing actual observed behaviors, both good and bad). Development of the Cultural Beliefs and Value statements and associated illustrative behaviors as part of the Core Ideology triad provides a verbal picture of the desired (i.e., appropriate and acceptable) behaviors. Ensuring the Core Ideology is aligned with the business strategy, focuses actions on the most important desired results. In essence, the strategy-aligned Core Ideology creates a verbal picture of a compelling, desired future state of organizational culture. What is required is a process to close the gap; taking the organization's culture from where it is today, to where it should be in the future.

Roger Connors and Tom Smith, in their seminal text *Change the Culture – Change the Game*,[11] outline in meticulous detail a process of changing organizational culture. An underlying premise is that changing culture requires:

- Prioritizing the actions that most contribute to the desired results

- Identifying the beliefs that generate the desired actions
- Providing experiences that instill the desired beliefs

The change process starts with creation of the 'experiences' in the workplace that will instill the desired beliefs, that drive the desired behaviors/actions (the new norms) to achieve the desired results. Continuing with the example above, assume that a desired result is Safety First as measured by 'no lost-time injuries or illness.' One behavior (action) required to achieve this result is using available machine guards. We suggested previously in this example that a prevalent belief might be that 'production is valued more than safety.' The question emerges, "What do workers need to 'experience' to change this belief (feeling), and instill the desired belief?

Reflecting on Fig. 4.1 above, the process for changing normative behaviors will start with creating new experiences in the workplace that change the beliefs underlying the undesirable behavior, instill new beliefs (e.g., safety and productivity are not mutually exclusive), which change work behaviors and results in the desired outcome (no lost-time injuries).

Moving Forward

A simplified 7-step framework to implement and maintain an intentional culture and enhance shared success drawn from multiple sources and personal experience is outlined below:

1. Create a plan

The plan should describe behaviors that are reflective of the desired Cultural Beliefs and Values, outline the workplace experiences that will instill the desired beliefs, include a timeline for introducing and reinforcing each experience, and establish a system to monitor progress.

2. Clearly define and routinely communicate Core Ideology

The desired message should be incorporated into onboarding and developmental training initiatives, described on company intranet sites and newsletters, and included in talking points for organizational meetings. To the extent achievable, a closed-loop communication process should be adopted that incorporates 'sending' the intended message, allows the 'receiver' to process and question the message, and assures the 'sender' that the intended message has actually been received.

3. Recruit, interview, and hire talent that fit into and will embrace the desired culture

Performance profiles used to advertise positions, cultural interviewing techniques, and targeted selection criteria (see chapter 13) should be incorporated into recruiting processes so that new talent introduced to the workplace are aware of expectations and aligned with and contribute to the desired culture.

4. Demonstrate Cultural Beliefs and (core and aspirational) Values in action, not just words

The environment people work in must be in alignment with stated cultural norms. This falls into the maxim – 'Walk the walk' if you are going to 'Talk the talk.' Avoid all instances where words say one thing, but actual experiences demonstrate something different.

5. Reinforce the desired culture through intentionally selected expected workplace behaviors

Part of workforce development should include observation, training, mentoring, and reinforcement of expected behaviors. Create a system of mutual accountability including how teams should hold each other accountable to embrace the agreed upon norms.

6. Highlight and draw attention to culture and recognize people for their contributions

Performance management processes (described in chapter 13), employee recognition programs, and public accolades should reinforce desired cultural norms. Consequences of nonconformance should also be established and enforced.

7. Monitor actual culture through casual conversations, strategy sessions, and formal surveys

The cultural assessment processes of culture walks, culture interviews, and culture surveys should not be 'one off' events. Instead, elements of these processes should be part of an ongoing business system of monitoring cultural and strategic alignment.

Summary

The premise for the Culture ingredient in our Recipe for Business Success is simple: Culture is at the heart of a company. If owning and operating successful organizations that are sustainable over time is your goal, setting and maintaining culture must be an ongoing initiative. In chapter 2 the components of the Core Ideology triad were introduced and the purpose each element plays in culture were explored. In chapter 3 example processes for developing the Core Purpose, Cultural Beliefs and Values, and Mission components on an intentional Core Ideology were outlined. And finally, in chapter 4, the basic neuroscience behind human behavior and a 7-step process for transitioning to a desired cultural destination were proposed. Taken collectively, the desired outcome is that after visiting offices, sales floors and field sites, attending conferences and meetings, observing interactions with customers, and assessing how your organization works together, an impartial organizational psychologist would witness and report strong conformance with your stated Core Ideology. When this is accomplished, the Culture ingredient will have been added to your unique Recipe for Business Success.

Chapter 5

TOP TAKEAWAYS AND TIPS

CASE STUDY - THE ASCEND SUMMIT LLC STORY

In 2018, I began working with the founders of ASCEND Summit LLC (ASCEND), a provider of top-tier indoor rock climbing in Pittsburgh, PA, in their efforts to formalize long-term goals and strategies following an exceptional first year in operation. At the conclusion of each Part, we'll follow their story to help illustrate the processes described in respective portions of *Recipe for Business Success*. As part of this chapter, we'll describe their journey to establish a core ideology.

When it came to formally plan for 2018 and beyond, the ASCEND leadership made the decision to conduct a planning workshop over two full-day sessions approximately five weeks apart. Several key considerations factored into this decision. This combination allowed the founders to:

- Dedicate adequate, uninterrupted time to planning,
- Prepare content needed during the workshop, and

- Reflect on outcomes drafted during the first session (e.g., core ideology, vision, and overarching goals) before progressing to the second session.

Since none of the elements of core ideology formally existed, and since core ideology underpins the strategic planning process (as will be described in Part II), the morning of the first day of our two-day workshop was dedicated to exploring the triad of core purpose, cultural beliefs and values, and mission.

As will be described further below, a consistent technique was followed during each workshop exercise. Each of the three founders was asked to individually engage in divergent thinking (creating a list of possibilities), followed by convergent thinking (narrowing their respective list), before drafting their initial responses. Each founder then shared their initial responses with the team, and common attributes were identified, culminating with development of a consensus outcome for each element.

Core Purpose

The first exercise involved development of a Core Purpose Statement. As suggested in Chapter 3: Defining Core Ideology, each founder was asked to create a list of attributes that characterize *Why we exist; what is our noble cause?* They then reviewed their respective lists and identified what they felt were the top three or four attributes. The founders shared their respective lists. In theory there could have been nine to twelve different attributes (i.e., three or four for each of the founders), but in practice there were only a handful, so the challenge was baking them into a singular statement. Following some debate, an initial Core Purpose Statement was drafted for their further consideration over the ensuing five weeks between sessions. Only slight changes were made. The resultant statement was:

To provide a healthy, lifestyle-based, alternative fitness experience in a climbing-focused and community-centered environment.

Cultural Beliefs and Values

The workshop progressed to the second element of the Core Ideology triad – cultural beliefs and values. A detailed discussion of cultural beliefs, similar to the information outlined in Chapter 2 – Elements of Core Ideology, followed. Once it was understood how culture assessments (i.e., culture walks, culture interviews, culture surveys) are required to uncover the deeply rooted beliefs that drive people's behavior and accepted norms, a decision was made to postpone development of this element. ASCEND had only been in existence for a little over a year, and while the founders worked diligently to create the desired environment for climbers and staff, it was simply too early to invest the resources (people, time, money) in conducting the necessary assessments to describe existing cultural beliefs. While that effort was intentionally postponed, attention shifted to the use of Value statements describing *How we behave.*

The exercise to identify the values that would become the foundational element of the ASCEND culture followed the process outlined in chapter 3. The founders were each asked to envision in their mind the name of 3 individuals (staff, investors, members) that fully embody what makes ASCEND great. They then listed traits shared by all 3 individuals on their own flip chart and posted their list of names and attributes on the wall. As a team they combined duplicate names, reviewed and consolidated similar traits, and ultimately retained those attributes shared by all of the exemplary individuals. Because of the early age of ASCEND, no significant effort was made to distinguish values that may have already existed in the work environment from those needed for the future. Instead, they recognized the need to formally introduce the outcomes as new Core Values and reinforce them with descriptions of desired behaviors. A set of 6 values was initially identified. With additional debate on the meaning of each attribute over the ensuing 5 weeks, a set of 4 values and their associated meaning emerged. The resultant value statements were:

Approachable – We are on the same level and we are all ears.

Authentic – We put ourselves, honestly and uniquely, into our work.

Passionate – We are actively engaged in the climbing lifestyle, deepening our understanding.

Hardworking – We value strong work ethics, while recognizing that people have different strengths.

Mission

The workshop progressed to the final element of the Core Ideology triad – Mission. This was likely the easiest exercise of the day as the founders had included a description of their mission in the business plan used to attract investors and commercial lenders. Nonetheless, the exercise progressed much as outlined in chapter 3. As part of the exercise, the team debated answers to the question *Why do our members and guests spend their resources with us?* The founders were each challenged to develop a list of attributes that:

- Described how ASCEND fulfills its Core Purpose
- Were externally oriented yet inspire staff to do their personal best
- Conveyed the human emotion and motivation of employees and customers

They then reviewed their respective lists and identified what each felt were the top 3 or 4 attributes. The founders shared their respective lists and identified common attributes that existed on all their lists. From those consensus attributes, a draft Mission statement emerged:

ASCEND fosters a holistic, community-based, climbing and fitness experience.

As planned, work on core ideology was completed during the morning session of the first day of the workshop. Breaks were incorporated to allow the managers to take care of any pressing matters. Otherwise, the time during the workshop was uninterrupted. The 'strawman' outcomes for Core Purpose, Core Values, and Mission were posted on the wall and discussed over lunch, before advancing to the next steps in the strategic planning process, which will be described as part of the ASCEND Story at the conclusion of Part II. A copy of the resultant ASCEND Strategic Plan incorporating this Core Ideology is included as Appendix 1.

Top 10 Takeaways from Part I

1. Culture represents the values, systems, attitudes, and set of assumptions that people in an organization share and adopt to achieve stated goals and objectives.

2. Some companies pay little attention to culture. Others create a picture of where they want to be and implement a strategy to establish and maintain a desired culture.

3. Regardless of which end of this spectrum an organization is on, they have the culture they deserve. That is, organizational culture is a choice.

4. Without an adequate, aligned, and supportive culture, developing and implementing strategy will be constrained.

5. Success is far more likely to occur when a relevant plan is aggressively implemented by an aligned and fully engaged workforce.

6. Culture and strategy are two parts of an integrated system. In practice, they must work together, in unison and harmony to achieve the best outcomes.

7. For the greatest opportunity for success, business strategy must be built upon an organization's culture, and organizational culture must be aligned with and supportive of the business strategy.

8. The Core Ideology that underlies culture is built upon 3 elements: core purpose, cultural beliefs and values, and mission, which establish *Why we exist, How we behave,* and *What we do,* respectively.

9. To change an existing culture requires creating experiences that influence peoples' beliefs and the underlying feelings and emotions that support those beliefs.

10. If organizational psychologists were to visit your company offices, field sites, and production floors, how would they describe how people work together to get things done?

Top 10 Tips for Implementing Part I

1. Don't be intimidated by the apparent complexity of designing and implementing an intentional culture. Address one component, then move on to the next.

2. Start with the top-down, 4-step process for establishing a core purpose statement outlined at the beginning of chapter 3.

3. Table (all or some of) the work on defining cultural beliefs if the effort involved in a cultural assessment (i.e., culture walks, culture interviews, and/or culture surveys) is too much initially. This work can be done later and used to enhance the fundamental efforts.

4. Select a group of influencers (people whose opinion and advice are respected and valued by many others within the organization, irrespective of positional authority) to complete the 8-step participative exercise outlined in chapter 3 to identify and define core and aspirational values.

5. Use this same group of influencers to complete the 3-step process of drafting a mission statement as described at the end of chapter 3.

6. Verify the draft core ideology (core purpose, beliefs and values, mission) is in alignment with the overall business strategy as described in the first section on chapter 4.

7. Follow the 7-step framework outlined at the end of chapter 4 to launch the cultural initiative with intent.

8. Establishing culture is not an event. If owning and operating a successful organization that is sustainable over time is the goal, maintaining culture must be an ongoing initiative.

9. Be certain that actions align with words; that actual behaviors match desired behaviors. Most importantly, as a leader if you are going to *talk the talk*, you must *walk the walk*.

10. Remember, no matter what else is going on, flying the airplane is always the number one priority. Don't take your eye off working in the business while working on the business.

Citations and References

Part I – Culture

1. Daniel Patrick Forrester, "Culture, Strategy and Harvard Business Review," Medium, May 28, 2016, https://medium.com/@dpforrester/culture-strategy-and-harvard-business-review-73e96c30729a#.pdkwbdkgvhttp://www.foxnews.com/opinion/2017/01/15/four-essential-lessons-general-james-mattis-taught-me-about-leadership.html; in response to Jay W. Lorsch and Emily McTague, "Change Is Not the Culprit," *Harvard Business Review*, April 2016, 96-105. https://hbr.org/2016/04/culture-is-not-the-culprit.

2. Simon Sinek, *Start with Why: How Great Leaders Inspire Everyone to Take Action* (New York: Portfolio, 2009).

3. Edgar Papke, *True Alignment: Linking Company Culture with Customer Experience for Extraordinary Results* (New York: AMACOM, 2014).

4. Jim Collins, *Good to Great: Why Some Companies Make the Leap...and Others Don't* (New York: HarperBusiness, 2001).

5. See Dominic Monkhouse, "What is Core Purpose in Business [and How Do you Find It?]," Blog, Monkhouse & Company, September 6, 2019, https://www.monkhouseandcompany.com/.

6. See "Core Purpose," Rhythm Systems, accessed February 4, 2023, https://www.rhythmsystems.com/defining-core-purpose.

7. See Susan M. Heathfield, "How to Understand Your Current Company Culture," LiveAbout, updated December 9, 2020, https://www.liveabout.com/how-to-understand-your-current-culture-1918811.

8. See Indeed Editorial Team, "Cultural Assessments: What They Are and How To Conduct One," Indeed, updated November 7, 2022, https://www.indeed.com/career-advice/career-development/cultural-assessment.

9. See "Netflix Culture – Seeking Excellence," Netflix Jobs, Netflix, accessed February 4, 2023, https://jobs.netflix.com/culture.

10. For additional information of Mission (and Vision) statements see Comparably, Inc.(website), https://www.comparably.com/; Mission Statement Academy (website), https://mission-statement.com/.

11. Travis Bradberry and Jean Greaves, *Emotional Intelligence 2.0* (San Diego: TalentSmart, 2009).

12. Roger Connors and Tom Smith, *Change the Culture, Change the Game: The Breakthrough Strategy for Energizing Your Organization and Creating Accountability for Results* (New York: Portfolio/Penguin, 2011).

Additional Resources

In addition to the specific sources outlined above, internet searches on the following topical headings will provide a wealth of additional information and insights on the topics discussed in Part I:

- Culture in business
- Core ideology in business
- Core purpose in business
- Cultural beliefs in business
- Cultural assessment in business
- Core values in business
- Mission statement in business

PART II
STRATEGY

Chapter 6

AN INTRODUCTION TO STRATEGY

Yogi Berra, a master of malapropisms, once quipped, "If you don't know where you are going, you might wind up somewhere else." This was one of his humorous distortions of the often-cited but also not-quite-accurate "if you don't know where you are going, any road will take you there" exchange between Alice and the Cheshire Cat in Lewis Carroll's classic children's tale, *Alice in Wonderland*.[1] In either case, the moral of the story is the same: if you don't know your desired destination, it's impossible to create a roadmap to get there. Put differently, it's best to start a journey with a destination in mind.

In the prologue we defined Strategy as the art and science of deploying resources to achieve stated goals or objectives of the organization (i.e., enterprise, business unit, or product/service line). Strategy requires a well-developed roadmap for getting to the desired destination, and this roadmap is frequently the outcome of a strategic planning process.

Strategy describes in broad terms how goals are to be achieved and marshals the resources (people, time, money) for their most efficient and effective use. As stated, strategy is frequently the outcome of a strategic planning process.

Alan Lakein, author of *How to Get Control of Your Time and Your Life*, suggests, "Planning is bringing the future into the present so that you can do something about it now."[2] He is also credited with the somewhat lighthearted expression of "failing to plan is planning to fail." Similarly, John Harvey Jones, best known for his BBC television show for struggling businesses, *Troubleshooter*, suggests, "The nicest thing about not planning is that failure comes as a complete surprise and is not preceded by a period of worry and depression."

Such humorous expressions notwithstanding, strategic planning and the resultant strategy are key determinants to success. The business imperative is simple—start with the destination in mind and develop a plan for getting there. Part II addresses this business imperative and includes a description of alternative methodologies of strategic planning in chapter 7, explores the elements of a suggested planning model in chapter 8, and outlines techniques and tools for implementing and maintaining an effective, ongoing strategic planning process in chapter 9, all with the aim of adding the Strategy ingredient to your unique Recipe for Business Success.

Chapter 7

STRATEGIC PLANNING PROCESSES

Dwight Eisenhower is quoted as saying, "Plans are worthless, but planning is everything." He went on to explain that details of a plan which were designed years in advance are often incorrect, but the planning process demands the thorough exploration of options and contingences. The knowledge gained during this probing is crucial to the selection of appropriate actions as future events unfold.[3] As such, any planning process for business should demand the thorough exploration of options and contingences and ensure a means to remain current so that informed decisions can be made as future events unfold.

Background Information

There is no singular, universally accepted definition of strategic planning. One source defines strategic planning as the art of formulating business strategies, implementing them, and evaluating their impact based upon organizational objectives. Another source suggests strategic planning is a process in which an organization's leaders define their vision for the future and identify their organization's goals and objectives, including the sequence those goals should be realized so that the organization can reach its stated vision. Most definitions center around the concept of an organization's process to define its direction and make decisions on allocating resources to pursue its strategy. After considering the merits and subtle differences of varying sources, the following definition emerged. For our purposes:

Strategic planning is an ongoing process that creates a roadmap for taking an organization from a well-defined Present State to a compelling and different Future State.

Strategic planning can be applied at an enterprise, business unit, or even on an individual product or services line of an organization. The "definition" of the process remains the same. There are, however, numerous models used to facilitate the strategic planning process. Conduct an internet search on "strategic planning process models," and an image of over a dozen planning models appears. Select "view all," and over a hundred illustrations of process models are presented.

For our discussion, all models have been grouped into one of two broad categories based upon a singularly important distinction (top-down vs cross-organizational). The names used to distinguish the two alternatives are simply labels. Don't read anything into the names. And don't assume that one is better than the other; the reality is each offers advantages and disadvantages.

Hierarchical (Longitudinal) Planning

In this group of processes, executive management with explicit responsibility for working 'on the business' identify overall strategic direction and long-term goals for the enterprise (with or without input from a board of directors or other key stakeholders). Operational leadership identifies objectives for their respective business units that are in alignment with and supportive of the long-term goal(s) identified by the executives. As illustrated below, the process cascades down through the organization and terminates with specific tactical objectives that are integrated as measurable metrics into individual employee expectations. Working from the bottom up, the concept is that when each employee accomplishes their respective objectives, their department will meet its objectives, the business unit will meet its objectives, and when all business units accomplish their objectives, the overall company goals will have been accomplished.

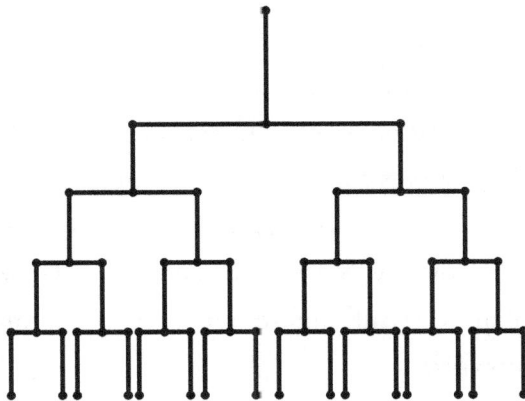

Executive Leadership

Operational Management

Front-Line Supervisors

Figure 7.1: Adapted from *One Mission* by Chris Fussell

Management By Objective (MBO) is one, perhaps the most recognized, example of a hierarchical planning process. The general steps in the MBO process are top-down and include:

1. Defining one or more long-term goals for the overall organization (by executive leadership)
2. Identifying business-unit-specific, shorter-term objectives (by operational management) that contribute to the longer-term organizational goals
3. Cascading business unit objectives down as expectations for individual employees (by front-line supervisors)

A more detailed discussion of MBO can be found in Adam Hayes article for Investopedia titled *Management by Objectives (MBO): Learn Its 5 Steps, Pros and Cons.*[4] For our purposes, the advantages of MBO (and other hierarchical models) are that managers work with employees to establish a short list of expectations that guide how an individual does their job (frequently called Key Result Areas or KRAs) that are related to the business unit objectives and supportive of the overall organizational goals. Disadvantages are that efforts become focused (sometimes solely) on what's measured, and groups/teams become (more) entrenched in their respective silos. MBO also results in distinct objectives within each business silo that when taken collectively can require significant resources (people, time, money) of the overall organization.

Cross-Organizational (Latitudinal) Planning

In this group of processes, executive management is frequently joined by other members of senior, operational, and front-line supervisors and other leaders in identifying overall direction and long-term goals. The resulting strategies cut horizontally across the organization. As illustrated by the circles below, frequently key influencers (those whose opinion and advice are respected and valued by many others within the work environment, irrespective of positional authority), are invited to participate in the organizational planning so that broad-based input is sought and advocacy for outcomes is encouraged.

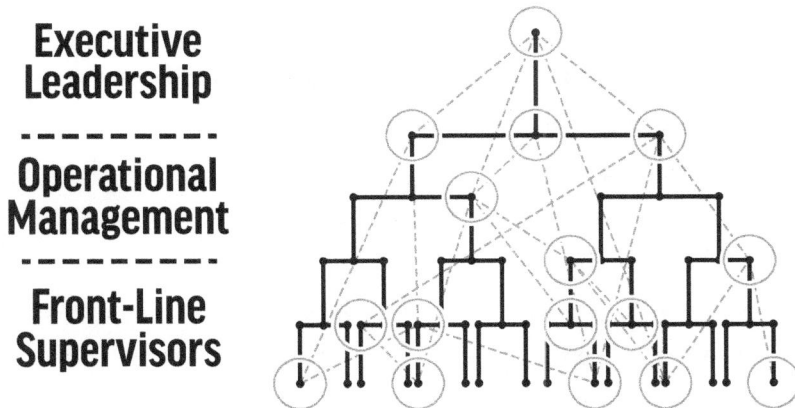

Executive Leadership

Operational Management

Front-Line Supervisors

Figure 7.2: Adapted from *One Mission* by Chris Fussell

Strategic Management is one example of this form of organizational planning. In its simplest sense, strategic management is the management of an organization's overall resources with the specific intent to achieve its collective longer-term goals and shorter-term objectives. The general steps in the strategic management process cut horizontally across an organization and include:

1. Defining long-term goals for the overall organization
2. Identifying shorter-term objectives for the entire organization that contribute to the longer-term goals

3. Creating diverse teams from across the organization to implement strategies

A more detailed discussion of strategic management can be found in Will Kento's article for Investopedia titled *What is Strategic Management.*[5] For our purposes, the advantages of strategic management include maximizing allocation of resources (people, time, money) and encouragement of cross-functional participation in improving targeted outcomes for the overall organization. Disadvantages include lack of clear line-of-sight for individual employee or work group contributions to the greater good. That is, it is more difficult for individual employees or work groups to see how what they do directly contributes to the cross-organizational goals.

In the hierarchical forms of strategic planning (like MBO), executives define overall goals, senior management at the operational level define shorter-term objectives for their respective business units, and these objectives are cascaded down to individual employee metrics. In the cross-organizational forms of strategic planning (like Strategic Management), diverse teams representing all business units and all levels of leadership work to identify both longer-term goals and shorter-term objectives for the entire organization, and cross-functional teams work on implementation. As indicated above, both forms of planning have advantages and disadvantages. However, there are hybrid models that attempt to leverage the advantages and mitigate the disadvantages of strict top-down or cross-organizational planning schemes.

Hybrid Models

By definition, a hybrid model employs elements of the top-down hierarchical scheme and the cross-organizational scheme. One such hybrid scheme starts with executives defining overall goals for the entire organization. But rather than delegate the balance of the planning process to operational units, the executive team also creates 1 or 2 enterprise-wide short-term strategic initiatives. A nuance is that this step typically involves recruiting diverse teams of Influencers from all operational units and all levels of leadership to work on these shorter-term objectives for the entire enterprise. Similarly, senior management at the operational level either define shorter-term objectives for their respective business (hierarchical) or recruit a team of Influencers from within their operational units (cross-organizational) to work on 1 to 3 shorter-term objectives for their area of responsibility (e.g., a business unit or staff function like human resources). This type of hybrid scheme may be advantageous for larger organizations, or mid-size organizations attempting to balance the emphasis and investment (people, time, money) between enterprise-wide initiatives with unit-specific initiatives.

Summary

Strategic Planning can be applied at an enterprise, business unit, or even on an individual product or service line of an organization. There are numerous models used to facilitate the strategic planning process. The range of models can generally be grouped into one of two broad categories based upon a singularly important distinction (top-down vs cross-organizational). Hybrid models also exist. These distinctions are not determinant in and of themselves. To the contrary, the intent is to recognize advantages and disadvantages of broad approaches to strategic planning so that intentional decisions can be made in selecting an optimum model for the organization. We will explore the elements of a flexible strategic planning model in chapter 8. This adaptable model can be applied in either a hierarchical, cross-organizational, or hybrid planning scheme. Help in deciding which planning scheme will work best in your organization (top-down, cross-organizational, or hybrid), and tools and techniques to conduct a strategic planning workshop and develop a strategic plan are addressed in chapter 9.

Chapter 8

A MODEL FOR STRATEGIC PLANNING

By our definition, strategic planning is an ongoing business process that results in a roadmap for moving an organization from a well-defined Present State to a compelling and different Future State. Strategy is a high-level plan for achieving one or more goals. Strategy is frequently the outcome of strategic planning. Our proposed model for strategic planning is illustrated on the next page.

As mentioned in chapter 7, there are many approaches to strategic planning. Fig. 8.1 illustrates a model that has been refined through application with both for-profit and not-for-profit organizations of varying size and complexity. It meets the needs for establishing the Strategy ingredient in our Recipe for Business Success and is flexible enough to be applied at the enterprise, business unit, or individual product/service level of an organization. It can also be applied in a hierarchical, cross-organizational, or hybrid scheme. Before exploring each of the elements in further detail, it is necessary to call attention to the "Core Ideology" component of the model.

Strategic Planning Model

Plan for Success

Key Strategic Initiatives

Present State

Current Initiatives

Survey Input

Analytics

SWOT

• Title • Objective • Definitions of Success

Implementation Plan

Review & Reload

Future State

Vision

Overarching Goals

CORE IDEOLOGY

Figure 8.1
With input from Arvind Paranjpe – Dynamic Leadership, Ltd.

As described in Part I, Core Ideology is the central element in the Culture ingredient in our Recipe for Business Success. Recall that culture and strategy are two parts of an integrated system. They must work together and in unison to achieve the best outcomes. Business strategy must be built upon a company's culture, and company culture must be aligned with and supportive of the business strategy. In our strategic planning model, Core Ideology underpins the strategic planning process and is the litmus test against which any resulting strategy should be judged.

As illustrated in Fig. 8.1, during the planning process participants listen to, analyze and debate data and information until reaching a common understanding of the *Present State* health of the organization. With this knowledge in hand, participants can create a verbal picture of a compelling and different *Future State*. In the center of the model, the *Plan for Success* outlines the roadmap to follow to move from the Present State to the desired Future State. It includes key strategic initiatives and associated definitions of success for the next year, a planning tool to identity and focus on the most important short-term tasks, and a review process that helps establish account-ability, monitor progress, and make course corrections as necessary. The concept behind each of these elements will be explored in this chapter. How to implement the model and conduct the necessary exercises to address each of these elements for a given organization is explored in chapter 9.

Present State

The first step in the strategic planning process is to establish a common understanding of the current health of the enterprise, specific business unit, or individual product/service line. Since participants in any strategic planning session come with varying knowledge and perspective, it is of critical importance to establish a mutual, collec-tive understanding of the present state of organizational health and the business environment. The entire strategic planning team should have a similar, shared set of facts that future discussions can be based. During the discussion of the *Present State*, participants consider the status of current strategic initiatives, survey input, and various ana-lytical data, before conducting a SWOT (Strengths, Weaknesses, Opportunities, Threats) analysis. Each of these components are briefly described below.

Current Initiatives

Whether explicitly defined, implicitly understood, or ad hoc, every business has some set of current initiatives that are designed to advance the organization. The point of this part of the exercise is to identify the current priorities for the enterprise, business unit, or product/service line, and the corresponding status of each initiative. For those elements of the business with existing plans in place, this involves an "After-Action Review" discussion (as illustrated in the sidebar and further described later) of the status of those specific initiatives. For those elements of the organization that do not have formal plans in place, this involves a more informal discussion of the projects on which each group has been working and the associated progress, or lack thereof.

Current Initiatives Year-End Action Review*

1. What was supposed to happen?
2. What actually happened?
3. Why was there a difference?
4. What can we learn from this?

*Bonus question at year-end:

5. What is required to bring this initiative to closure.

Survey Input

In strategic planning, survey studies generally involve the collection and analysis of responses to questions or observations used to gain insights from various stakeholders. Surveys can range from structured design, collection and analysis of responses solicited from targeted groups, to focus group meetings or personal one-on-one interviews, to general discussions among the strategic planning participants. In all instances, the purpose is to gain insights that will be of value to strategic planning participants in assessing the *Present State* health of the organization and the markets it serves.

The list of possible groups to survey in the sidebar is illustrative only, and not considered exhaustive. And not all sources of input are created equal. For instance, surveys of employees and customers are frequently (but not always) of far greater value than input from vendors or suppliers. Regardless, the goal of any survey should be to compile and consider relevant input from others not directly engaged in the strategic planning process (i.e.,

Survey Input

- Employees
- Customers/Members
- Vendors/Suppliers
- Impacted Parties
- Professional Associations
- Government Agencies
- Other Stakeholders

'not in the room') that will be of value to the actual strategic planning participants (i.e., those 'in the room'). This input can be valuable in establishing baseline metrics of organizational health (e.g., employee engagement, customer satisfaction, etc.) or providing alternative perspectives on varying aspects of the company, its markets, and associated strengths, weaknesses, opportunities, and threats.

Analytics

Discussions of analytics generally deal with more objective, quantitative data than the more subjective, qualitative input from surveys. Information on the following might be considered:

- Operating & Financial Data
- Key Performance Indicators; Key Result Areas; or Critical Success Factors
- Organizational Structure and Processes
- Quality Management System Findings
- Health & Safety Performance

- Demographic Data – internal (employee) and/or external (customer)
- Competitive Analysis
- Environmental Factors
  □ Domestic and international geopolitics
  □ Macro- and micro-economics
  □ Industry and technology trends

Like Surveys, the list of possible Analytics to consider is illustrative only, and not exhaustive. And like surveys, not all analytic data is of equal value. For instance, depending upon circumstances, detailed financial data or analysis of competition may be of far greater value to participants than discussions of organizational structure. In any case, it is doubtful any strategic planning session will have the luxury, let alone the capacity, to compile and consider all the survey and analytical data described above. The litmus test for establishing the actual information and data to be presented is quite simple; *What is the minimum information required so that all participants have a sufficient, mutual understanding of the current state of organizational health and business environment to plan for the future?*

What is the minimum information required so that all participants have a sufficient, mutual understanding of the current state of organizational health and business environment to plan for the future?

SWOT Analysis

The technique of SWOT analysis is quite common but by no means intuitive. Its utility during strategic planning occurs only when the exercise of identifying the top Strengths, Weaknesses, Opportunities, and Threats is conducted after all participants have considered the status of current initiatives, survey input, and analytics described above. When conducting their SWOT Analysis, participants must look at all the information from the proper perspective.

- Strengths & Weaknesses represent an internal point of view (looking in the mirror). What does the organization excel at that separates it from its competitors (Strengths) or needs to improve upon to perform at its optimum (Weaknesses)?
- Opportunities & Threats represent a point of view of the external environment (looking out the windshield). What are the favorable external factors that offer a competitive advantage (Opportunities) and factors that have the potential to harm the organization (Threats)?

It is not unusual for the evaluation of the present state of organization to take up the single largest block of time in a strategic planning workshop. It is time well spent. This process allows a diverse group of participants to have a singular, collective understanding of the *Present State* of organizational health of an enterprise, business unit, or product/service line and associated business environment. The essential 'deliverable' from the present state discussions are the outcomes from the SWOT Analysis. That is, all the discussion of the progress made on current initiatives, the review of input from various surveys, and consideration of essential analytics is distilled down to a shortlist of top Strengths, Weaknesses, Opportunities, and Threats for the organization. The outcomes of the SWOT Analysis create a guide or framework to help participants explore the *Future State.*

All the discussion of the progress made on current initiatives, the review of input from various surveys, and consideration of essential analytics is distilled down to a shortlist of top Strengths, Weaknesses, Opportunities, and Threats for the organization .

Future State

Strategic Planning is an ongoing process that provides a roadmap for taking us from a well-defined *Present State* to a compelling and different *Future State;* i.e., the desired destination. There are two essential components of the *Future State*, a Vision statement, and long-term Overarching Goals. Each of these components are briefly described below.

Vision Statement

The vision statement starts to paint a verbal picture of the future by describing *What we want to become?* A vision statement should convey an idealistic picture of the future to employees and other interested stakeholders. It should be inspirational – motivating employees to be engaged for the common good – and aspirational – a timeless ideal never

Vision

• Answers the question *What do we want to become?*
• Should convey aspirations for the future to employees and stakeholders
• Must be clear, concise and compelling

to be fully realized (i.e., the proverbial 'carrot on the end of a stick'). As such, a vision statement is not subject to frequent revision. An effective vision statement is clear, concise, and compelling. Examples of a few recognizable vision statements include:[6]

- **Amazon:** To be earth's most customer-centric company, where customers can find and discover anything they might want to buy online.
- **Avon:** To be the company that best understands and satisfies the product, service, and self-fulfillment needs of women—globally.
- **Ben & Jerry's:** Making the best ice cream in the nicest possible way.
- **Nordstrom:** To serve our customers better, to always be relevant in their lives, and to form lifelong relationships.
- **Starbucks:** To establish Starbucks as the premier purveyor of the finest coffee in the world while maintaining our uncompromising principles while we grow.
- **Walmart:** To be the destination for customers to save money, no matter how they want to shop.

Overarching Goals

The second component of the Future State involves the creation of a more definitive and objective description of the desired destination. *Overarching Goals* create a specific, measurable, and attainable verbal picture of what the enterprise, business unit, or product/service will look like at some specific point in the future. Overarching Goals must be timebound. Set goals too close in the future and there is little distinction from current initiatives. Set goals too far off in the future and the environment will most certainly have changed.

A 3-5-year window is suggested for most organizations. It allows enough time to accomplish compelling and significant change, but not so far in the future that circumstances dramatically differ from the envisioned environment used as the basis for the goals.

An example of a hypothetical overarching goal an insurance carrier might establish as a long-term goal:

Phantom Insurance:

Writes $X million in annual property coverage premium in the 6-state New England market, with an overall loss ratio of < Y% across the book of business.

As stated previously, we will describe a process to help form a unique vision statement and longer-term overarching goals for an organization in chapter 9.

Plan for Success

The elements of the strategic planning model discussed thus far have all been developed with a singular outcome in mind; to create a shared picture of a compelling and different destination. The next step is to create the *roadmap* for going from the *Present State* (characterized by the SWOT Analysis) to the desired *Future State* (characterized by the Vision statement and Overarching Goals).

The Plan for Success roadmap will define how goals are to be achieved and marshal resources (people, time, money) for their most efficient and effective use. As illustrated in Fig. 8.1 strategic planning model above, the Plan for Success has three elements: Key Strategic Initiatives, Implementation Plans, and Review & Reload sessions. Each of these components are briefly described below.

Key Strategic Initiatives

Perhaps some have heard the quote from Patrick Lencioni, prolific author and founder of The Table Group, *"If everything is important, then nothing is."* With a clear picture of our destination in mind (i.e., where we want to be in 3 to 5 years), participants can focus on establishing the few, most important priorities for the next year. The question asked is simple:

> *Based upon our Present State of organizational health, what are the (3-5) most important things we need to focus on in the next 12 months, that are consistent with our Vision and move us towards our longer-term Overarching Goals?*

Once debated, the answers to this question become the Key Strategic Initiatives (or Key Strategies) for the year. We have previously defined "strategy" as a high-level plan for achieving desired goals or objectives. In our Recipe for Business Success, there are 3 components of each key strategy: a title, a business objective, and definitions of success.

Title – provides a 1-2-word label for the main idea or area of focus for each key strategy.

Objective – provides a common understanding of what the title means and is a succinct statement that describes the outcome to be achieved.

Definitions of Success – provide the specific, measurable results that must be achieved to accomplish the objective. Definitions of Success for each Key Strategy must answer the question:

What must be true one year (12 months) from now, for us to be able to look back and say with any credibility, that we were successful with this key strategy?

Taken in combination, an example of a key strategy (title, objective, and definitions of success) for a hypothetical provider of professional arial and underwater drone services might look like:

KS-'23-1 – Market Diversification

Objective – to identify, evaluate, and prioritize adjacent market sectors for expansion of existing drone services.

We will know we have been successful when, by December 2023, we have:

a. Researched, selected, and utilized market research tools to identify at least 5 potential market sectors for further assessment;

b. Used lean canvas, competitive analysis, and other assessment tools to fully characterize the magnitude of opportunity in each identified market sector;

c. Drafted go-to-market strategies, including cost estimates and return-on-investment analysis, for the top 3 identified markets; and

d. Initiated implementation per approved go-to-market strategies for at least 1 new market sector.

Key Strategies establish in specific, measurable terms what must be accomplished in the next 12 months, to move one year closer to achieving long-term *Overarching Goals*. Key Strategies must be broken down even further into tactical plans to help ensure continual progress is made and allow for adjusting tactics as circumstances evolve. That is where the Implementation Plan comes in.

Implementation Plan

The term Implementation Plan refers to a specific tool illustrated in Figure 8.2 below. Other project planning tools (e.g., MS Planner, Monday.com, Wrike, Kantata, etc.) might be used to manage and track progress. For now, the concept behind the tool is what is important.

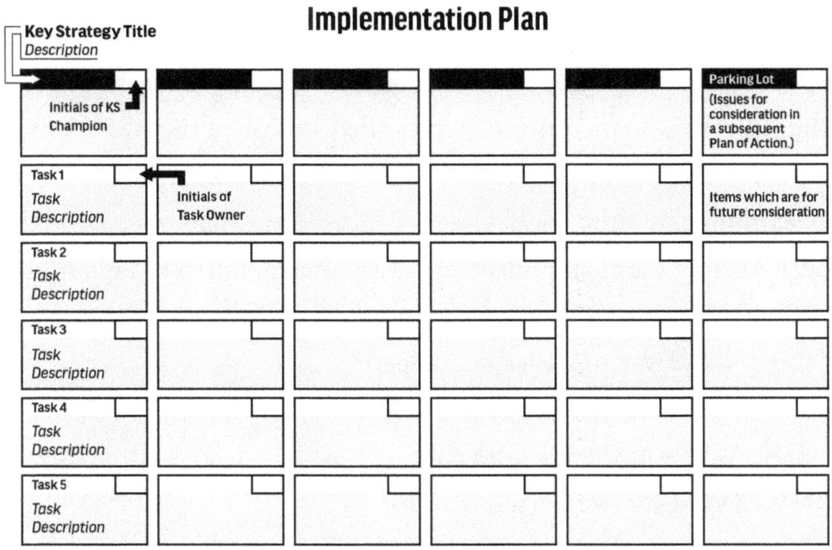

Figure 8.2: Spreadsheet-based planning tool

Thus far the strategic planning process has helped create a timeless Vision statement and specific Overarching Goals for 3-5-years out. The Key Strategic Initiatives and associated Definitions of Success describe outcomes that must be true in the next 12 months to move towards achieving those longer-term Overarching Goals. The Implementation Plan breaks down the annual Key Strategies even further, into 90-day increments.

The Implementation Plan process helps establish the specific tasks that must be initiated and/or completed in the next 90 days to move towards meeting the annualized Definitions of Success for each Key Strategy. The process for completing and using the Implementation Plan is described in chapter 9.

Review & Reload

The third and final component of the Plan for Success roadmap is the Review & Reload (R&R) session. The R&R session helps ensure plans get converted to action. An R&R session should be scheduled at the end of each 90-day cycle from the initial strategic planning workshop. The R&R session incorporates a modified version of the After-Action Review (AAR) process developed by the military as a way for everyone to learn quickly from soldiers' experiences in the field. As part of the R&R session, the champion of each Key Strategy answers 4 questions:

- What was supposed to happen?
- What actually happened?
- Why was there a difference?
- What can we learn from this?

After the discussion of the After-Action Review outcomes with the entire strategic planning group, the tasks on the Implementation Plan for the next 90-day cycle are discussed, including a description of how the tasks move the Key Strategy team closer to its year-end Definitions of Success. Completed tasks from the current 90-day cycle are dropped and new ones, as appropriate, are added. As described, the R&R process keeps things moving forward and promotes account-ability, but also allows for course corrections as circumstances change.

This completes our review of each of the elements of the strategic planning model as illustrated in Fig. 8.1.

Optional Elements

As indicated in the beginning of chapter 7, there are many models for strategic planning and no attempt is being made to inventory every approach, let alone assess their nuances. There are, however, two specific elements enough strategic planning practitioners are incorporating into the process to warrant further exploration. These include defining a North Star as a celestial compass for an organiza-tion and/or identifying what Patrick Lencioni calls a "Thematic Goal" that focuses all short-term key strategic initiatives.[7] Let me start by noting that I don't feel either of the 2 optional items are essential for conducting productive strategic planning or the creation of effective strategic plans. Instances where they may add value are described in the narrative to follow.

North Star

Like earlier days of strategic planning when Vision and Mission were frequently misused until the jargon became more standardized, the concept and uses of "North Star" are evolving. One line of usage suggests a product or service-based tactical strategy to maximize delivery by focusing on a singular metric for each product or service (called the North Star Metric). This use of the concept is close enough to well established metrics like Key Performance Indicators to diminish the need for further discussion. However, "North Star" is also being used to introduce another element to the overall strategic planning model. Larger organizations that adopt a hierarchical planning scheme and want to establish overall direction for the total enterprise, but allow individual business units to develop their own strategic plans, may create a "North Star" that resides in the *Future State* element of the model illustrated in Fig. 8.1.

When considering incorporating a North Star element into the model, it is worthwhile to consider the classical use of the phrase:

> The North Star is the anchor of the northern sky. It is a landmark, or sky marker, that helps those who follow it determine direction as it glows brightly to guide and lead toward a purposeful destination. It also has a symbolic meaning, for the North Star depicts a beacon of inspiration and hope to many.

Jargon (e.g., Purpose, Values, Mission, Vision, Goals, etc.) are terms of art that take on specific meaning when used in a strategic planning context. To the extent possible, this jargon should be broadly understood by all those engaged in developing and implementing strategic plans. Therefore, it will be critically important to fit North Star within the existing jargon (terms of art) associated with the strategic planning process.

If adopting the classical use of the term "North Star" as an anchor and guiding light, it seems appropriate that the element would be added in the verbal description of the *Future State*, between the timeless, qualitative Vision statement and quantitative long-term Overarching Goals. The North Star statement should be directional, providing guidance to and ensuring all goals lead to the desired destination. For instance, a technology company might use "Industrial Revolution 4.0 Readiness" as its North Star to provide direction to all its business units.

Thematic Goal

Similar to how North Star is used as a bridge between the Vision and Overarching Goals in the verbal picture of the desired Future State, some practitioners incorporate a Thematic Goal within the Plan for Success. The Thematic Goal is designed to rally employees around a common cause and to create an anchor or singular theme that unites all Key Strategic Initiatives for the following year. For instance, a nationwide retailer might establish a thematic goal of "World Class Customer Satisfaction," to emphasize the thread that unites all its short-term key strategic initiatives.

If both North Star and Thematic Goal elements were added, the resultant model would look as follows:

Strategic Planning Model

Plan for Success

Present State	Thematic Goal	Future State
Current Initiatives	Key Strategic Initiatives ⬇	Vision
Survey Input	Implementation Plan ⬇	North Star
Analytics	Review & Reload	Overarching Goals
SWOT		

CORE IDEOLOGY

Figure 8.3: Expanded strategic planning model

Whether either or both optional elements are added to the adopted model for strategic planning should be determined in part by decisions on how the Plan is to be communicated among the stakeholders. That is, the North Star and the Thematic Goal serve to provide notional direction, rallying cries, and anchors for the long-term goals and annual key strategies, respectively. The effort involved in creating and communicating a North Star statement and/or Thematic Goal may be of value for large, multi-division organizations. However, the complexity added to the strategic planning process and the investment required in communication to capitalize on the 'rallying cry' may not be warranted for a small or mid-market organization. Specific guidance on developing North Star statements and Thematic Goals is included in chapter 9.

Summary

The strategic planning process illustrated in Fig. 8.1 starts with a deep exploration of the Present State organizational health and business environment of the enterprise, business unit, or a product/service line, culminating in a thorough SWOT Analysis of current Strengths, Weaknesses, Opportunities, and Threats. As described below, there is a diminishing timeline associated with the resulting strategic plan, that moves from the timeless nature of an aspirational vision to the highly specific tasks of a 90-day tactical plan.

The Strategic Plan itself starts with a timeless, aspirational *Vision* statement. *Overarching Goals* lend definition to the Vision by describing in specific terms the challenging goals to be accomplished over the ensuing 3 to 5 years. *Key Strategic Initiatives, Implementation Plan,* and *Review & Reload* elements (collective known as the Plan for Success), provide the roadmap, or Strategy, for getting from where you are now to where you want to be. They break long-term goals down into increasingly smaller pieces that are manageable (i.e., 3-5-year goals, 12-month key strategic initiatives, 90-day tactical plans, and R&R sessions). It's like the metaphorical question, *How do you eat an elephant?* The answer is, *One bite at a time.*

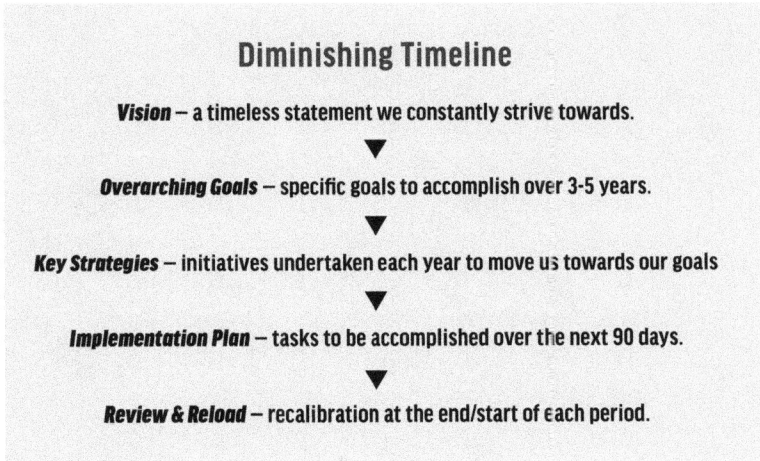

Diminishing Timeline

Vision – a timeless statement we constantly strive towards.

▼

Overarching Goals – specific goals to accomplish over 3-5 years.

▼

Key Strategies – initiatives undertaken each year to move us towards our goals

▼

Implementation Plan – tasks to be accomplished over the next 90 days.

▼

Review & Reload – recalibration at the end/start of each period.

One of the frequent criticisms of strategic plans is that a lot of work goes into developing them, only to sit on the shelf and collect dust. This never should occur if it is recognized that Strategic Planning is an *ongoing process* – not an event. When strategic planning becomes an event, rather than an ongoing process, it fails. The process of developing a strategic plan is the subject of the next chapter. The ongoing implementation of the strategic planning process and execution of its resultant strategies are described in Chapter 14: Executing on Strategy.

Chapter 9

DEVELOPING A STRATEGIC PLAN

The goal of strategic planning should be the development, implementation, and maintenance of an effective and efficient strategy. The words effective and efficient can both mean "capable of producing a result," but there is an important difference. Management guru Peter Drucker once said, "Efficiency is concerned with doing things right. Effectiveness is doing the right things."[8] Drucker goes on to suggest, "There is surely nothing quite so useless as doing with great efficiency what should not be done at all." The imperative is clear. The process for strategic planning must be both efficient—i.e., *doing things right* by producing desired results without wasting resources—and effective—i.e., *doing the right things* by focusing resources on achieving the most important results.

Preparation

The planning model outlined in chapter 8 starts with people getting together and sharing insights about the present. During these meetings, people make decisions about the future based upon those insights. The key to being effective and achieving desired results involves people converting those decisions into actions. And for the process to be most efficient, the results of the actions must be monitored and shared, and then redefined as circumstances warrant. The linchpin in this circular and unending process is "people." The first consideration in developing a strategic plan should be answering the question, *Who should participate in the process?*

Participants

Selection of participants in a hierarchical (longitudinal) top-down strategic planning process as presented in the illustration below from chapter 7 is relatively straight forward.

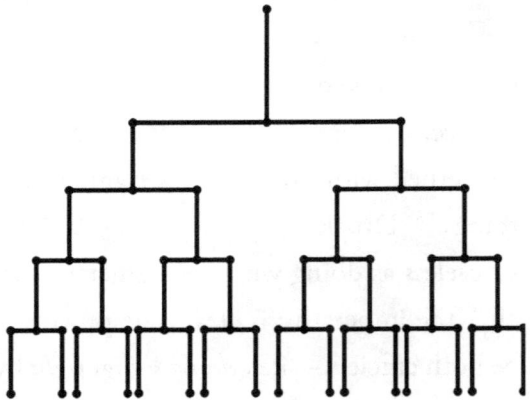

Executive Leadership

Operational Management

Front-Line Supervisors

In the hierarchical scheme, those executive and senior managers who have organization-wide roles that include strategy-related responsibilities should participate. The work of this team includes all the work involved with assessing the Present State of organizational health,

SWOT analysis, and the resultant development of the Vision and Overarching Goals for the entire enterprise. In cascading these goals down into the organization, teams of operational and front-line supervisors take on responsibility for developing the Plan for Success for their respective business units (or product or service groups). The resulting Key Strategic Initiatives are used by managers to establish Key Result Areas as individual performance metrics for their respective staff.

The hierarchical scheme of planning is perhaps most applicable in larger organizations where executive leadership sets overall direction and operational managers create unique strategies for their business units that are supportive of and in alignment with the executives' goals. Alternatively, it might be embraced in organizations with Stable, Control, Results-Oriented, or Compete cultures (as described in chapter 4).

Selection of participants in a cross-organizational (latitudinal) strategic planning process as presented in the illustration below from chapter 7 is more complex.

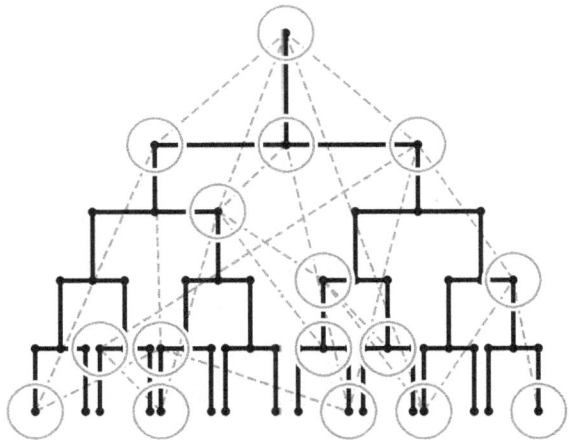

Executive Leadership

- - - - - - - - -

Operational Management

- - - - - - - - -

Front-Line Supervisors

The cross-organizational scheme of planning is perhaps most applicable in small to mid-size organizations where leadership from all organizational levels creates strategies for the overall organization. Alternatively, it might be embraced in organizations with Creative, Innovative, Expertise, or Participative cultures (as described in chapter 4). In either case, participants should be selected from among the key influencers in the organization (illustrated by circles in Fig. 7.2 above). For our purposes, organizational "Influencers" are those whose opinion and advice are respected and valued by many others within the work environment, irrespective of positional authority, including those working in differing business units and functions.

From within this group of Influencers, participants should be selected with a goal of gaining cognitive diversity. That is, selecting a variety of open-minded people with different insights, ideas, judgement, and thought processes. This is frequently achieved by focusing on surrogates of diversity such as age, gender, discipline or role, and business or operating unit. But the end goal should always be a diversity of perspective and problem-solving skills that will contribute to an engaging strategic planning workshop.

Hybrid planning schemes rely on a combination of hierarchical, top-down planning for selected elements in the overall process, in combination with cross-organizational planning for others. In these scenarios, the appropriate management team completes the top-down planning elements while a team of Influencers completes the cross-organizational elements. In the example described in chapter 7, one such hybrid scheme starts with executives defining overall goals for the entire organization. Rather than delegate the balance of the planning process to operational units, the executive team also creates 1 or 2 enterprise-wide short-term strategic initiatives. A nuance is that this step typically involves recruiting a diverse team of Influencers from all operational units and all levels of leadership to work on the shorter-term objectives for the entire enterprise.

Senior management at the operational level either define shorter-term objectives for their respective business (hierarchical) or recruit a team of Influencers from within their operational units (cross-organizational) to work on 1 to 3 shorter-term objectives for their area of responsibility (e.g., a business unit or staff function like human resources). This type of hybrid scheme may be advantageous for larger organizations, or mid-size organizations attempting to balance the emphasis or resources (people, time, money) invested in enterprise-wide initiatives with unit-specific initiatives.

In either the hierarchical, cross-organizational, or hybrid schemes, the total number of participants should be large enough to create a robust planning environment while still encouraging engagement from all participants. For smaller organizations, a minimum of three or four key participants can be effective if they bring enough cognitive diversity, and everyone's opinions are truly valued. As the organization grows, a maximum of 24 to 28 participants is suggested. This allows participants to be divided into 4 manageable teams (of 6 or 7 each) for many of the planning exercises to be described later (e.g., SWOT analysis). Being part of an ongoing strategic planning process requires a substantive time commitment. Regardless of size, minimum expectations of participants should be established to maximize use of this time. All participants should be required to:

- Thoroughly prepare for the workshop by completing any pre-session assignments
- Actively participate in all discussions and exercises during the workshop
- Meaningfully engage with and contribute to key strategy teams
- Prepare for and participate in quarterly Review & Reload sessions

Experience has shown that some participants in strategic planning workshops have been selected solely based upon their position (on the org chart) and without the requisite commitment (as outlined in the bullet points above). A degree of caution is warranted. At best, a passively disengaged (e.g., silent) participant wastes their own and everyone else's time. They take a seat at the table from a possible contributor. An actively disengaged (e.g., cynical) participant damages the teamwork environment and can undermine the overall process with their negativity. Only those who will actively engage in the workshop and participate in the implementation of the resulting plans should participate in the process, regardless of position.

There should also be 'rules of engagement' during the actual strategic planning workshop to fully realize the benefit of cognitive diversity. All participants should:

- Take their 'hats' off at the door, focusing solely on the good of the organization, not their respective turfs.
- Be serious about their perspective (without becoming zealots) and avoid deferring to authority. All participants are the same rank.

- Demonstrate the trust and mutual respect necessary for free conversations.
- Be open-minded, recognizing the aim cf argument should be progress, not victory.

The guidance above should help determine how to intentionally select participants for the strategic planning workshop. But there is another group of individuals who may not be participants in the workshop, but who arguably should have input into the overall strategic planning process.

Board of Directors

It is widely held under state law that boards have a duty to act in a manner that they reasonably believe is in the best interest of the corporation. "Best interests of the corporation" is a term of art that is generally understood to mean acting for the benefit of the share-holders and of the company as-a-whole. As stated in a post by Ross Pounds for Diligent titled *The Roles and Responsibilities of a Board of Directors* "The main role of a board of directors is to perform the duties of strategic planning and oversight."[9] To meet these responsibilities, boards are expected to govern the corporation by broad policies and practices such as:

- Shaping the strategic direction of the organization
- Holding the CEO and management of the organization responsible for establishing the strategic plan
- Challenging, approving, and monitoring implementation of the strategic plan

> **If a Strategic Envisioning workshop involving an organization's board of directors is not a productive option, the workshop can, and arguably should be conducted among the executive leadership team before initiating strategic planning.**

One approach to fulfilling these obligations in what has been characterized as an era of exponential rate of change (i.e., Industrial Revolution 4.0) is participation in a Strategic Envisioning workshop

Most recognize that it is impossible to predict the future. In his 1963 book *Inventing the Future,* Nobel Prize winner Dennis Gabor noted "The future cannot be predicted, but futures can be invented."[9] Instead of attempting to predict, envisioning involves picturing in the mind, or imagining the possibilities. As used herein, Strategic Envisioning involves a systematic process of imagining future possibilities and provides notional direction to the strategic planning process. Note that if a Strategic Envisioning workshop involving an organization's board of directors is not a viable or productive option, the workshop can, and arguably should be conducted among the executive leadership team before initiating strategic planning.

STRATEGIC ENVISIONING WORKSHOP

Peter Drucker once said "The important and difficult job is never to find the right answer; it is to find the right question." Albert Einstein suggested "If I were given one hour to save the planet, I would spend 59 minutes defining the problem and one minute resolving it." And Thomas Watson, the founder of IBM, said, "The ability to ask the right question is more than half the battle of finding the answer." The common thread of all these and numerous other observations is the fundamental importance of asking good questions. [10, 11, 12, 13]

Our version of Strategic Envisioning involves a systematic process of imagining future possibilities by brainstorming for questions that provide notional direction to the strategic planning process. Numerous techniques have been offered as effective brainstorming techniques. Many of the techniques seek to identify the right questions to ask. Kaihan Krippendorff reported on a 4-step method to breakthrough ideas used by Chris Gentile as manager of R&D efforts of new technologies that have generated over $5.2 billion in retail sales.[14] Step 1 is to Change the question. Hal Gregersen, in his seminal book *Questions are the Answer,*[15] asserts that questions direct our information search and all but determine (preordain) the answer. Step 2 of his 3-step Question Burst process is to Generate the questions.

The 5-Step Strategic Envisioning session outlined below draws upon these and other brainstorming techniques to uncover what Gregersen characterizes as Catalytic Questions - that fully 'reframe' the problem and provide new angles for solving it. Before beginning strategic envisioning, board members or senior leadership must be exposed to much of the same Present State information as participants in the actual strategic planning workshop so that they have a strong understanding of organizational health and the business environment. With this as background, participants can begin to 'imagine future possibilities.'

STEP 1 – CLIMATE SETTING

The goal of *Climate Setting* is to set the tone for a safe and effective environment for exploration of ideas. After review and discussion of pertinent parts of the Present State information and data, it can be helpful to introduce a dream as part of climate setting for the envisioning session. Ask the participants to relax and envision it is 5 to 10 years from the present. They are guests at the largest, most prestigious banquet of industry peers. Our organization has just received an Industry Excellence Award. What industry forum are we attending? Ask the participants to imagine what the speaker says to explain why our organization deserves such high honors and recognition. Consider how the speaker describes what our organization does, and the characteristics of the organization that make it outstanding in achieving its aims. Challenge the participants to keep that vision alive as they complete each of the Strategic Envisioning exercises.

STEP 2 – DIVERGENT THINKING

Divergent thinking is a creative process of generating original ideas and possibilities (e.g., brainstorming for questions). Ask the participants to collectively create a list of 20 or more questions that need to be addressed in order to provide direction and create a compelling vision of the Company for the future. Before starting the exercise, explain the ground rules:

- No preambles or other positioning statements
- No judging, debating, or answering any question
- Don't speak over each other
- You have 5 minutes…

The 5-minute limit helps create a sense of urgency yet is long enough for the group to develop 20 or so questions. Have someone record each question as close to verbatim as possible. A form for collection of and processing of responses during each step in a strategic envisioning workshop is attached as Appendix 2.1.

STEP 3 – CONVERGENT THINKING

Convergent thinking is the process of focusing efforts on finding the best suited solutions from a range of options, or in this instance, the best outcomes of the brainstorming in step 2. To do so, each participant should individually identify their top 3 questions from the 'top 20' list of questions. Then as a group, create a tally of the preferred choices and narrow the field to the top 5 questions.

STEP 4 – REFRAME THE QUESTION(S)

Reframing the question is a powerful technique described by Gregersen. He suggests that questions are the frame into which answers will fall. By **reframing** the question, the range of possible solutions dramatically changes. Gregersen offers numerous examples of reframing questions, one of which is summarized below:

A group of parents in New Jersey were feeling stuck for solutions. Their kids, whose autism spectrum disorders made it difficult for them to function independently, were about to age out of the program provided through the local school system. Conversations among the parents kept landing on their biggest worry: "What will happen to our children when we are not around?" They felt trapped and made little progress until they reframed the question to ask "What can we do to make sure our child has a purposeful life?" The simple shift in language opened new channels and motivated productive action.

Ask participants to study the top 5 questions and be on the lookout for questions that suggest new pathways. Task them to create one or two new Catalytic Questions that fully 'reframe' the problem and provide new angles for solving it.

STEP 5 – FINALIZE THE CATALYTIC QUESTION(S)

Ask the participants to unpack and expand the reframed questions using the "5 whys." Ask why the chosen question seemed important. Then ask why that reason seemed important, and so on five times. Review all the responses and identify "What catalytic questions do we really need to answer?" where catalytic questions are defined as those questions specifically framed to dissolve barriers to creative thinking and channel pursuit of solutions into new pathways.

Strategic planning participants must then process the catalytic questions as part of the Future State discussions (described later in this chapter).

As an example, the board of directors for KTA-Tator, Inc followed the 5-Step process outlined above. The outcomes were then vetted by executive and senior management prior to inclusion in the forthcoming strategic planning workshop. The resultant catalytic question was:

How do we transform our business to be more *Agile** in pursuit of our Vision, to take advantage of opportunities and mitigate threats created in the [post-Covid] new normal and 4th Industrial Revolution (IR4)?

*Where "Agile" means:

The organizational capacity to effectively detect, assess, and respond to environmental changes in ways that are purposeful, decisive, and grounded in the will to win.[16]

With participants for the strategic planning workshop selected and input (catalytic questions) from the board or executive leadership obtained, the process of developing a strategic plan can be initiated. The strategic planning process starts with the creation of a common and shared understanding of the present state of organizational health of the enterprise and the business environment.

Present State

The sidebar highlights the topical content discussed in chapter 8 that might be considered as part of the Present State discussions during a strategic planning workshop. As previously suggested, the litmus test for establishing what should actually be presented is quite simple; *What is the minimum information and data required so that all participants have a sufficient, mutual understanding of the current state of organizational health and business environment to plan for the future?*

Current Initiatives
- Status of Key Strategic Initiatives

Survey Input
- Employees
- Customers/Members
- Impacted Parties
- Professional Associations
- Other Stakeholders

Analytics
- Operating & Financial Data
- Key Performance Indicators
- Organizational Structure and Processes
- Quality Management System Findings
- Health & Safety Performance
- Demographic Data
- Competitive Analysis
- Environmental Factors

Depending upon the scope of Present State information to be considered, it may be advisable to provide the materials as a pre-session assignment in combination with a meeting in advance of the actual workshop. The advance meeting is necessary to allow all participants the opportunity to ask *clarifying questions* about the Present State information. That is, since the intent is to establish a common set of factual information and data that can be relied upon, all questions should be directed at clarifying the information as opposed to debating its meaning. Determining the implications of all the Present State information is the underlying purpose of the SWOT analysis.

SWOT Analysis

The SWOT analysis is the first exercise of a strategic planning workshop. Establishing 4 teams (of 1 or more participants each) is desirable so that each team can concentrate on one attribute (i.e., Strengths, Weaknesses, Opportunities, or Threats) of the analysis. When there are multiple participants on a team, members should be selected to gain cognitive diversity, using age, gender, discipline or role, and business or operating unit as surrogates. Pairing anyone with direct reporting relationships should be avoided so as not to potentially hinder full engagement.

Each of the 4 teams should be assigned one attribute and tasked with identifying the organization's top 5 Strengths, Weaknesses, Opportunities, or Threats (as assigned), based upon all the Present State information and data presented. Recalling from chapter 8, when conducting their SWOT Analysis, participants must look at all the information from the proper perspective.

- Strengths & Weaknesses represent an internal point of view (looking in the mirror). What does the organization excel at that separates it from its competitors (Strengths) or needs to improve upon to perform at its optimum (Weaknesses)?
- Opportunities & Threats represent a point of view of the external environment (looking out the windshield). What are the favorable external factors that offer a competitive advantage (Opportunities) and factors that have the potential to harm the organization (Threats)?

Each team should present and debate their conclusions with the entire strategic planning group. Keeping in mind the maxim *If everything is important, then nothing is*, the entire group should focus attention on what is most important by agreeing upon the top five (no more than seven) attributes of Strengths, Weaknesses, Opportunities, and Threats. In addition to being recorded for future use, the results should be 'left on the wall' (literally) for visibility and reference during the balance of the workshop.

Future State

With a grounded, shared understanding of the Present State of organizational health and business environment, attention can be directed to developing the verbal picture of a compelling and different Future State. At the start of the Future State discussions, the strategic planning group should be presented with and challenge the catalytic questions (if the Strategic Envisioning process was adopted). The goal should be to identify and pursue new pathways to find potential solutions suggested by these questions as participants address the elements of Future State (i.e., Vision, North Star, and Overarching Goals).

Addressing each of these three potential elements of the Future State involves a similar process. Each team (the same teams used during the SWOT Analysis) should carry out the breakout session assignments described below for each element, with all team responses presented and debated among the full strategic planning group. Each element should be addressed in sequence.

Vision

As described in chapter 8, a clear and concise Vision statement outlines the ideal being pursued. It is inspirational, while establishing the aspirations for what you want to become. As a timeless statement, it will not be subject to frequent revision. Crafting such a compelling statement will be challenging, especially when done by a committee. Nonetheless, getting input from the strategic planning team is essential to developing a meaningful statement (or revising an existing statement) that will be embraced across the organization.

Each of the four teams should use divergent thinking (e.g., brainstorming) to identify the range of key attributes that might be addressed within their draft Vision statement. Once an exhaustive list of attributes is developed, each team should use convergent thinking to narrow the list and identify the top 3-5 attributes they collectively feel are most important.

With these key attributes in mind, each team should prepare an initial draft Vison statement.

The draft statements developed by each of the four teams should be presented and debated among the entire strategic planning group. The entire group should repeat the 2-step process above, this time identifying the top 3-5 attributes common to the collection of initial draft statements. Once completed, a singular 'strawman' Vision statement can be created. (Recall the example vision statements in chapter 8.) It will be subject to review and final editing by executive management but will provide enough notional direction to describe "*What we want to become*" to guide completion of the remaining elements of the Future State.

North Star (Optional)

The first question to consider is whether a North Star will be an element of the organization's verbal description of the desired Future State. The arguments surrounding this element were previously outlined in chapter 8 and won't be repeated here. There are two approaches to take if the decision is made (usually by executive management) to establish a North Star. If the primary purpose of the North Star statement is to *glow brightly to guide and lead toward a purposeful destination*, it should be developed *before* considering the Overarching Goals for the next 3-5 years so that it can provide notional direction. If on the other hand, the primary purpose of the North Star statement is as an *anchor, landmark, or sky marker that is a beacon of inspiration,* it should be developed *after* establishing the Overarching Goals so that it can provide the rallying point for their pursuit. In either case, the process for developing the 'strawman' North Star statement should be essentially identical to the process described immediately above for the Vision statement.

Overarching Goals

This step is arguably the most important element of the Future State. Goals will be developed which create an objective and quantifiable picture of the organization 3-5-years out. The Overarching Goals will describe the destination used to guide development of the roadmap or strategy for getting there. This will be a 3-part exercise.

Step 1 - Divergent Thinking (brainstorming the range of options)

Based upon their assessment of the SWOT Analysis and in consideration of any catalytic questions, each of the breakout teams should be tasked to identify the top 5 areas of targeted improvement of vital importance to the organization's success [frequently referred to as key result areas (KRAs) or critical success factors (CSFs)] that must be addressed in the selected long-term (3-5 year) timeframe. The list must move the organization towards and embody the strawman Vision described previously.

Step 2 - Convergent Thinking (narrowing the range of options)

Each team should present their list of top 5 KRAs/CSFs to the group. The entire strategic planning group should then debate and narrow the list to a collectively agreed top 3 to 5 KRAs/CSFs essential to moving the organization forward.

Step 3 - Draft Goals and Metrics

This step can be completed as a group, or each team can be assigned one of the outcomes of Step 2 to further process. The objective of Step 3 is to create goals, written in the present tense, imperative mood as if they have already been achieved. In 1981, George T. Doran coined the acronym SMART.[17] There have been many derivations of the meaning of the acronym. For our purposes, each goal should be **S**pecific – written so that others not involved in the strategic planning process will understand the destination. It should be **M**easurable – there should be no debate about what constitutes success. The goal statement may incorporate or be followed by the metrics that will be monitored and used to assess success. The measures of success must be **A**chievable – in the agreed upon 3-5-year **T**imeframe. And naturally, the goals must be **R**elevant to achieving the Top KRAs/CSFs identified in Step 2. Recall from chapter 8 the example of a hypothetical overarching goal an insurance carrier might establish:

Phantom Insurance:

Writes $X million in annual property coverage premium in the 6-state New England market, with an overall loss ratio of < Y% across the book of business.

Collectively, the 3-5 Overarching (SMART) Goals should create a verbal picture of the compelling and different Future State to be achieved. The next phase of the strategic planning workshop (sometimes held at a subsequent date to allow time to process the outcomes of the Future State) will be to develop the *roadmap for getting from where you are to where you want to be.*

Plan for Success

This is the step in the strategic planning model where the process deviates within the hierarchical and cross-organizational schemes. For those adopting a hierarchical (longitudinal) top-down model of strategic planning (e.g., large organizations or those that embrace Stable, Control, Results-Oriented, or Compete cultures), the executive leadership team provides the elements of the Future State to the business/operating units to initiate the process of cascading objectives down into the organization. As such, the Plan for Success portion of the workshop would be conducted separately within each business/operating unit. For those adopting a cross-organizational (latitudinal) model (e.g., small or mid-size organizations or those that embrace Creative, Innovative, Expertise, or Participative cultures), the same team of strategic planning participants (influencers) that developed the Future State (Vision and Overarching Goals) will develop a Plan for Success that cuts across the entire organization.

The sidebar highlights the topical content discussed in chapter 8 that might be considered as part of the Plan for Success discussions during a strategic planning workshop. Collectively, these elements represent the roadmap, or strategy, for taking us from the well-defined Present State summarized in the SWOT Analysis, to the compelling and different Future State defined by the Overarching Goals. Each element is discussed below.

Plan for Success

Thematic Goal

Key Strategic Initiatives

- Title
- Objective
- Definitions of Success

Implementation Plan

- Planning Tool

Review and Reload

- Process

Thematic Goal (Optional)

Like the optional North Star, the first question to consider is whether a Thematic Goal will be an element of the Plan for Success. The arguments surrounding this element were previously outlined in chapter 8 and won't be repeated here. There are two approaches to take if the decision is made (usually by the strategic planning team) to establish a Thematic Goal. If the primary purpose of the Thematic Goal statement is *a common cause that takes precedence over all others*, it should be developed *before* considering the Key Strategic Initiatives for the next year (12 months). If on the other hand, the primary purpose of the Thematic Goal is as *a singular theme that unites all key strategic initiatives,* it should be developed *after* they have been developed so that the Thematic Goal can provide the rallying point for their pursuit.

In either case, each of the breakout teams should be asked to answer the question *"If we accomplish only one thing in the next 12 months, what would it be?* Because of the purpose served, Thematic Goals are usually limited to a few-word catch phrase. All draft statements should be presented individually and debated by the entire strategic planning group. The entire group should define the final Thematic Goal.

Key Strategic Initiatives

The concept behind establishment of annual (12 month) key strategic initiatives was outlined in chapter 8. Once again, each of the breakout teams should be tasked to identify the 3-5 objectives that need to be accomplished in the next 12 months to move towards the longer-term (3-5-year) Overarching Goals. And like each of the breakout sessions described above, each team should present their list to the group. In keeping with the maxim *If everything is important, then nothing is,* after the individual teams have presented their findings, the entire group of strategic planning participants should narrow the list to no more than 5 key strategies for the ensuing 12 months. The group should create a 1 or 2-word title and short description of the envisioned key strategy, and a champion or co-champions to the initiative should be identified. This is where the work of the full strategic planning group ends.

The first task for the champion or co-champions of each key strategy is to recruit additional staff to join their respective key strategy (KS) team, usually with relevant subject matter expertise and interest in the topical area. The first task of the KS team is to finalize the Title, Objective and Definitions of Success for each key strategy. As introduced in chapter 8:

Title – provides the 1-2-word label for the main idea or area of focus for each key strategy.

Objective – provides a common understanding of what the title means and is a succinct statement that describes the outcome to be achieved.

Definitions of Success – provide the specific, measurable results that must be achieved to accomplish the objective. Definitions of Success for each Key Strategy must answer the question:

What must be true one year (12 months) from now, for us to be able to look back and say with any credibility, that we were successful with this key strategy?

Each Key Strategy team should create 3-5 specific measures of success outlined in a fashion similar to:

We will know we have been successful when, by xx/yy/zzzz, we have:
1. *Xxx*
2. *Yyy*
3. *Zzz*
4. *Etc.*

These *Definitions of Success* establish in specific, measurable terms what must be accomplished in the next 12 months, to move one year closer to achieving the *Overarching Goals*. Each KS team then breaks down the annual goals into the tasks that must be accomplished in the first/next 90-days. That is where the Implementation Plan comes in.

Implementation Plan

As presented in chapter 8, the Implementation Plan is a spreadsheet-based tool utilized to break down annual Key Strategic initiatives even further, into 3-5 specific tasks that need to be accomplished during each 90-day cycle. The concept is simple: completion of bite-size tasks over each 90-day cycle moves teams closer to the 12-month *Definitions of Success* established for each Key Strategy. And when the *Definitions of Success* for each Key Strategic Initiative are accomplished for the year, the organization moves one step closer to accomplishing the longer-term (3-5-year) Overarching Goals.

The overall Implementation Plan (see Fig 8.2) tool involves a series of spreadsheets built within a workbook. Each tab in the workbook includes the Implementation Plan for one 90-day cycle. Each spreadsheet has 6 columns, with 1 column used for each Key

Strategy, and one assigned as a Parking Lot. As illustrated in Figure 9.1, the title and objective of the Key Strategy appears in the header for each column. Each header is followed by 5 task cells that constitute the tactical Plan of Action for a given cycle. For each column, specific tasks that must be initiated and/or completed during the upcoming 90-day cycle are described. Accomplishing these tasks moves the team towards success.

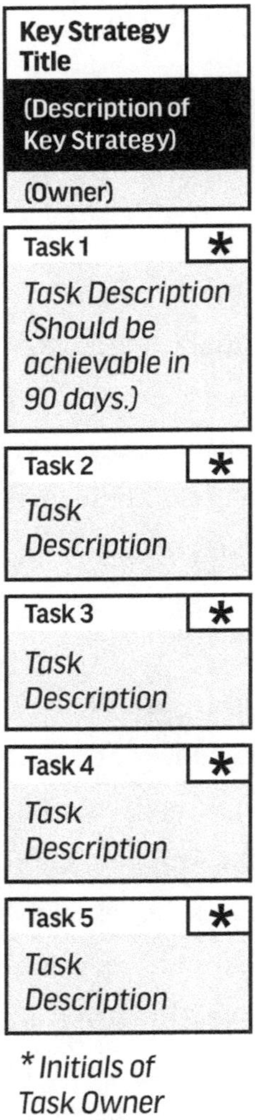

Key Strategy Title	
(Description of Key Strategy)	
(Owner)	

Task 1	*
Task Description (Should be achievable in 90 days.)	

Task 2	*
Task Description	

Task 3	*
Task Description	

Task 4	*
Task Description	

Task 5	*
Task Description	

* Initials of Task Owner

Fig 9.1: KS tasks

After the tasks are entered (for all Key Strategies), it is time to step back and assess the overall Implementation Plan for reasonableness. Remember the expression, "*If everything is important, then nothing is!*" The final litmus test is simple – the Plan of Action for all Key Strategies must be **A**chievable with available resources (people, time, money) – that is, all tasks must be completed or at a minimum, work must be initiated, within the next cycle of 90 days.

The champion of each Key Strategy volunteers to oversee all aspects of execution, and schedules calls or meetings with team members on an as-needed basis. Each task should also have the initials of the 'owner' of that specific task. In this manner, the key strategy team develops the plan of action for the next 90 days, each key strategy has a "champion" to help ensure overall success, and each task has a leader (i.e., the owner) to get the work done.

Note, this portion of the strategic planning is frequently completed outside of the strategic planning workshop. If that is the case, it is essential that KS teams be assembled, Definitions of Success established, and the first 90-day Implementation Plan be developed within 1-3 weeks of the strategic planning workshop to maintain momentum and to initiate work on the key strategies in a timely manner.

Review & Reload

One final item to address before the end of the strategic planning workshop is to establish Review & Reload (R&R) sessions for approximately 90, 180, and 270 days following the workshop. Prior to each R&R meeting, the champion of each Key Strategy color-codes each task within their plan of action in accordance with the following key.:

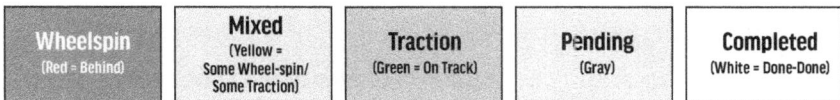

Wheelspin	Mixed	Traction	Pending	Completed
(Red = Behind)	(Yellow = Some Wheel-spin/ Some Traction)	(Green = On Track)	(Gray)	(White = Done-Done)

Figure 9.2: Progress assessment key

The background for each task is colored Grey when originally placed on the Implementation Plan (indicating that work is pending). Prior to the R&R session, each task is colored White if it is completed, Green if it is still in progress but on schedule, Red if work hasn't begun or progress is well behind schedule, or Yellow if work has started but has not progressed to the desired point.

During the R&R session the champion of each KS answers our 4 After- Action Review questions:

- What was supposed to happen?

- What actually happened?
- Why was there a difference?
- What can we learn from this?

After debating all the responses with the entire strategic planning team, the champion proposes a Plan of Action (i.e., one column of the Implementation Plan) with proposed tasks for the next 90 days. The group challenges the tasks, always focused on achieving the agreed upon Definitions of Success for the respective key strategy by the end of the planning year. As suggested previously, the R&R process promotes accountability, helps monitor progress, and allows for course corrections as events unfold. It also helps ensure that strategic planning remains an ongoing process, and not an event.

Summary

Part II was designed to include a description of alternative methodologies of strategic planning in chapter 7, explore the elements of a flexible planning model in chapter 8, and outline suggested techniques and tools for conducting an effective strategic planning process in chapter 9. All this was with the aim of adding the Strategy ingredient to your Recipe for Business Success. One task remains: communicating the Strategic Plan to the balance of the organization.

Some companies go to great lengths to create a visually appealing and illustrated version of their strategic plan. A template for a basic format is provided in Appendix 2.2. It is a simple, narrative presentation. Graphics and marketing specialists might be engaged to translate the narrative into a single-page graphical presentation for widespread stakeholder distribution. Regardless of the format used, the more challenging issue is closing the communication loop. This requires the sender creating the message, determining how it will be delivered to the receiver, and how the receiver can engage in probing and questioning so that feedback can be obtained to ensure the intended message was received.[18] Developing an intentional communication campaign is essential to gaining support for the Plan across the organization.

The Facilitator

There is one final question to consider before progressing to Part III on Execution. That is, who should facilitate the strategic planning process? A "facilitator" is *one that helps to bring about an outcome by providing indirect or unobtrusive assistance, guidance, or supervision*. In strategic planning, the four key roles of a facilitator are to:

1. Manage the process – ensuring engagement and balanced participation of all participants
2. Manage the clock – ensuring a sense of urgency with energy focused on the topic at hand
3. Bring about resolution – ending prolonged debates, spurring debate when dialogue wanes
4. Focusing on the outcome - avoiding tangents and rabbit holes, moving towards conclusion

Consideration should be given to internal and external facilitators. Both have advantages and disadvantages. A facilitator from inside the organization, perhaps from a training department, may have the right facilitation skills but lack the level of respect required to lead participants that have greater organizational authority. The CEO or other executive may also have the requisite facilitation skills but suffer from positional authority that may limit participant engagement.

A professional facilitator from outside the organization should have all the requisite skills but may lack specific knowledge of the business and the markets it serves. All options can be successful. The best decision will require intentional consideration of fully defined advantages and disadvantages given the specific circumstances at hand.

Chapter 10

TOP TAKEAWAYS AND TIPS

CASE STUDY – THE ASCEND SUMMIT LLC STORY

I n 2018, in the midst of ASCEND's first strategic planning workshop, we developed "strawman" outcomes for Core Purpose, Core Values, and Mission during the morning session on day one of two full-day sessions. These outcomes were posted on the wall and discussed over lunch.

With Core Ideology in place, the next step was to gain a common understanding of what strategic planning was all about. We had conducted a "Strategic Planning 101" orientation before the workshop so that the founders could question the process and evaluate its efficacy. Our discussions provided the opportunity to explore each of the elements of the strategic planning model (as illustrated in Fig 8.1 of Chapter 8: A Model for Strategic Planning) and discuss the resources (people, time, money) required to develop and implement a longer-term strategy. This was an important part of the buy-in required to make the process work. It also helped the founders conclude that they would be the only participants in the strategic planning process. Without labeling it, they were adopting a hierarchical, top-down planning scheme, which was appropriate given the limited experience of the balance of the management team (i.e., ASCEND Pittsburgh had only been open a little over a year) and the practical desire to fully explore any long-term goals with the Board of Managers before engaging staff.

Present State

One advantage of being an entrepreneurial start-up is that the three founders were all well-grounded in most all issues of organizational health and the business environment. That is, while each had specific areas of responsibility where they led team efforts, they all shared an awareness in most areas of operation.

Current Initiatives

Not surprisingly, there were no formal key strategic initiatives from the prior year to review. All the effort during the first year of operation was focused on launching the enterprise and creating the associated business processes like finance and accounting, recruiting and onboarding, operations and maintenance, customer experience, and marketing. While there were no explicit current initiatives to review, each founder informally addressed key developments in their respective areas of responsibility.

Survey Input

It was also not surprising that there were no formal surveys of stakeholder input during the first year of operation. Instead of reviewing actual survey results, the founders were asked to ponder questions about a hypothetical survey including:

- Who would the responses be from,
- What questions would have been asked, and
- What might the answers say about the Present State?

The discussions also focused on identifying areas where survey input from targeted stakeholders would help frame the conversation for subsequent years of the ongoing strategic planning process. Any key concepts that emerged from this combination exercise were captured on flip charts and posted on the wall.

Analytics

Because we had completed a 'strategic planning 101' session preceding the actual workshop, the managers were each able to assemble reports on their respective areas of operation. Since the participants in the workshop were limited to the three founders, it was not difficult to establish a mutual, collective understanding of the present state of organizational health and the business environment. This portion of the workshop included a series of short presentations and discussions to ensure the founders shared a common understanding of:

- Operating and financial performance
- Member and community demographics
- Status of organizational structure (leadership development) and
- Current business processes

The breadth and depth of analytics that were addressed would change in later years (described at the conclusion of Part III on Execution) as other staff were invited to participate in the process.

SWOT Analysis

The Present State portion of the workshop concluded with a SWOT analysis exercise wherein the team collectively brainstormed a list of attributes, then challenged the results to identify their consensus top 5 Strengths, Weaknesses, Opportunities and Threats. The resulting SWOT Analysis contained confidential information and therefore won't be reproduced. However, it should be noted that in addition to posting the outcomes on the wall for reference during the balance of the afternoon discussion of the Future State, the outcomes were recorded and appended to the resulting Strategic Plan so that they might be challenged and revised in subsequent years.

Future State

With a grounded, shared understanding of the Present State of organizational health and business environment, attention was directed to developing the verbal picture of a compelling and different Future State. Due to the start-up nature of ASCEND and the need for efficient use of resources (people, time, money), no effort was invested in a strategic envisioning exercise or development of a North Star. Instead, all energy was focused on the two essential elements of the Future State – development of a Vision statement and Overarching Goals.

Vision

As part of the workshop, the challenges of creating a clear and concise vision statement were discussed. The resulting vision was to outline the timeless ideal being pursued, and was to be both inspirational for all stakeholders, as well as aspirational by decreeing what the founders wanted ASCEND to become. While challenging, crafting such a compelling statement followed the same technique of divergent and convergent exercises.

Each of the founders was asked to create a list of key attributes that might be addressed within their draft vision statement. Once an exhaustive list of attributes was developed, each founder was asked to identify the top 3 or 4 attributes from their respective list. Since there were only three founders involved, we skipped the step of preparing individual versions of a draft vison statement. Instead, each member described their top attributes to the team and explained why they had selected them.

In theory there could have been as many as 9-12 attributes to consider. In practice there were fewer, but this did not diminish the challenge for the team in crafting an initial draft vision statement. In fact, the 'strawman' Vision for ASCEND created during the workshop was substantively revised during the 5 weeks between workshop sessions. The resulting Vision statement was:

> *ASCEND is nationally recognized as an industry influencer, integrating leading edge technology, equipment, and programming to provide access to all climbing disciplines, while serving as the most inclusive employer and fitness community in the markets we serve.*

The initial 'strawman' Vision statement was used as the backdrop for development of long-term goals.

Overarching Goals

This was perhaps the most engaging portion of the workshop because consideration of long-term plans had not received the level of conversation among the team that current issues demanded. Clearly, all the founders had considered future possibilities, but none of these ideas were as fully vetted by the team as we would do during the following exercise. Before embarking on the next exercise, the team debated how far out in time their goals should stretch. They all envisioned a reasonably rapid rate of change and felt a shorter duration was warranted.

In the end they determined their Strategic Plan would provide the roadmap for taking ASCEND from where it was in May 2018 to just after its 5-year anniversary in May 2022, a 4-year long-term planning horizon (long enough to effect change, but short enough that the assumptions under which the plan was developed would remain reasonably valid).

Once again, we started the process with a divergent thinking exercise. Based upon the outcomes of the SWOT Analysis that were posted on the wall, each founder was tasked to identify a list of key result areas they might address to capitalize on their Strengths, overcome their Weaknesses, realize their Opportunities, and/or mitigate their Threats. They were then asked to narrow their respective list by identifying the most important key result areas on their respective lists that must be addressed to move the organization forward towards the strawman Vision. The team shared their list of key result areas and quickly agreed upon the 5 most important areas of focus. The next step involved agreeing upon a 1- or 2-word label and associated metrics of success for each area. The final step was to transform each area as a verbal description of what ASCEND would look like in 4 years, but written in the present tense, imperative mood as if they had already been achieved. The resulting Overarching Goals for May 2022 were:

Growth/Expansion

- ASCEND has three or four full-service facilities in Southwestern PA operating with acceptable financial performance and possesses an evaluation model to assess growth options in real time.

Operational Excellence

- ASCEND has achieved operational excellence by way of consistently implemented systems and processes reflected in well-defined job functions throughout the company.

Competitive Youth Program and Circuit

- ASCEND has spearheaded and fosters a robust regional youth climbing competition circuit, rooted in schools, communities, and private groups.

Expanded Outdoor Program

- ASCEND operates a seasonal outdoor guiding program, leading regional day trips, weekend excursions, and all-inclusive retreats.

Foundation/Philanthropy

- ASCEND has a philanthropic arm that operates independently to provide financial support to local organizations that fall within specific funding areas, all while providing additional marketing opportunities for the ASCEND brand.

Collectively, the five Overarching Goals provided a verbal picture of the compelling and different Future State to be achieved. The next phase of the strategic planning workshop would involve developing the roadmap [Plan for Success] for getting from where they were to where they wanted to be.

As indicated previously, this second session was scheduled for about five weeks later. This allowed the founders to review, challenge, and edit the strawman statements of Core Ideology, Vision, and Overarching Goals. As designed, a significant portion of the second day of the strategic planning workshop was set aside to establish consensus on any proposed edits and reaffirm their combined commitment to these essential pieces of the Strategic Plan (i.e. Core Ideology, Vision, and Overarching Goals). With these finalized elements in hand, and the outcomes of the SWOT Analysis posted on the wall, we progressed to the creation of the roadmap.

Plan for Success

While it was introduced during the 'strategic planning 101' session, the concept behind establishment of annual key strategic initiatives (as outlined in chapter 8) was reviewed. Each founder was then asked to answer the following question:

> Based upon our Present State of organizational health, what are the three to five most important things we need to focus on in the next 12 months, that are consistent with our Vision and move us towards our longer-term Overarching Goals?

Unlike previous brainstorming exercises where the range of possibilities was described, this exercise required limiting options to only those initiatives of greatest importance in the next 12 months. Each founder presented their list to the team. The team narrowed the list to 5 topical areas to pursue during the ensuing 12 months. Once debated, the outcomes became the Key Strategic Initiatives (or Key Strategies). As described in Chapter 9: Developing a Strategic Plan, the team defined three components for each key strategy: a title, a business objective, and definitions of success.

> Title – provides a 1-2-word label for the main idea or area of focus for each key strategy.

> Objective – provides a common understanding of what the title means and is a succinct statement that describes the outcome to be achieved.

> Definitions of Success – provide the specific, measurable results that must be achieved to accomplish the objective. Definitions of Success for each Key Strategy must answer the question:

> *What must be true one year (12 months) from now, for us to be able to look back and say with any credibility, that we were successful with this key strategy?*

The final key strategies (KS) contained confidential information and therefore will not be re-stated here. However, it can be said that the key strategies all revolved around expansion, operational excellence, and youth and outdoor programing. The team recognized the opportunity, if not the need, to engage other members of ASCEND leadership to participate in implementing the key strategic initiatives. One of the founders was identified as the "Management Owner" for each KS. In addition, the Management Owner agreed to recruit a "Board Champion" to provide counsel during the implementation phase. And the three founders collectively agreed upon names of other key leaders who would be recruited to serve on each team. In the end, the decision to be more inclusive expanded the range of participants in Review & Reload (R&R) sessions and subsequent annual planning workshops.

The newly formed KS teams determined the tasks to be completed in the first 90 days and the Management Owner entered the tasks in their respective column on the Implementation Plan. Initially there were issues of duplication of effort in some overlapping areas, but these were resolved before or during the R&R sessions. The productivity of the R&R sessions, and specifically the After-Action Review discussions, increased as the broader set of participants came to appreciate the open and non-judgmental environment the founders embraced. The R&R sessions were repeated on a scheduled 90-day basis with little deviation from the process outlined in chapter 9. A copy of the resultant ASCEND Strategic Plan is included as Appendix 1.

Top 10 Takeaways from Part II

1. It's best to start every journey with a destination in mind.
2. Strategy is the art and science of deploying resources (people, time, money) to achieve stated goals or objectives of the organization.
3. Strategic planning is a business process that results in a strategy for pursuing identified goals - a roadmap for moving from a well-defined present state to a compelling and different future state.

4. Business strategy must be built upon a company's culture, and company culture must be aligned with and supportive of the business strategy. Core Ideology underpins the strategic planning process and is a litmus test against which any resulting strategy should be judged.

5. During the planning process participants listen to, analyze, and debate progress on current initiatives, information from surveys of various stakeholders and analytical data, before conducting a SWOT (Strengths, Weaknesses, Opportunities, Threats) analysis, to reach a common understanding of the *Present State* health of the organization.

6. With knowledge of the present state of organizational health and business environment in hand, participants can create a verbal picture of a compelling and different *Future State*, including a Vision statement and long-term (3-5 year) Overarching Goals.

7. The *Plan for Success* provides the roadmap to follow to move from the *Present State* to the desired *Future State*. It includes key strategic initiatives and associated definitions of success for the next 12 months, a planning tool to identity and focus on the most important short-term tasks, and a 90-day review process that helps establish accountability, monitor progress, and make course corrections as necessary.

8. Strategic Envisioning involves a systematic process of imagining future possibilities and provides notional direction to the strategic planning process.

9. "Efficiency is doing things right; effectiveness is doing the right things." Strategic planning is efficient – doing things right by producing desired results without wasting resources;

and effective – doing the right things by focusing resources on achieving the most important results.

10. Make all long-term overarching goals and short-tern key strategic initiatives SMART: **S**pecific, **M**easurable, **A**chievable, **R**elevant, and **T**imebound.

Top 10 Tips for Implementing Part II

1. There are numerous models and methods for conducting strategic planning. It is far better to focus your attention on the desired outcome (i.e., creation of a roadmap) and adopt those techniques that fit your organization. Don't be a slave to any singular methodology.

2. The hierarchical scheme of planning is perhaps most applicable in larger organizations where executive leadership sets overall direction and operational managers create unique strategies for their respective business units that are supportive of and in alignment with the overall direction. Alternatively, it might be embraced in organizations with Stable, Control, Results-Oriented, or Compete cultures (as described in chapter 4).

3. The cross-organizational scheme of planning is perhaps most applicable in small to mid-size organizations where leadership from all organizational levels create strategies for the overall organization. Alternatively, it might be embraced in organizations with Creative, Innovative, Expertise, or Participative cultures (as described in chapter 4).

4. The distinction between the broad categories of strategic planning (i.e., hierarchical vs. cross-organizational) are fundamentally rooted in two things: the nature of the partici-

pants involved (e.g., senior executives vs. key influencers), and the breadth of their focus (i.e., the broader organization vs. a singular business unit).

5. In the end, a hybrid approach may be best, wherein senior executive create the overarching goals for the enterprise and 1 or 2 cross-organizational key strategies, and operational management recruits influencers from among their team to create key strategies for the business unit.

6. A full initial strategic planning session typically requires the better part of 2 days. Some have found it far more productive and participant-friendly to hold the workshop over 3 shorter (3-4 hour) sessions, as follows:

   a. Present State – process all present state information and data and complete the SWOT analysis

   b. Future State – process any catalytic questions and develop vision and north star statements, and long-term (3-5 year) overarching goals

   c. Plan for Success – create a thematic goal, and identify the key strategic initiatives for the next year (12 months)

7. For discussion of the present state, determine the minimum information required so that all participants have a sufficient, mutual understanding of the current state of organizational health and business environment to plan for the future.

8. When possible, use 4 teams (of 1 or more participants each) to complete each strategic planning exercise. The technique followed for all workshop exercises follows a similar pattern – teams engage in divergent thinking (brainstorming), followed by convergent thinking (identifying what is most

important), culminating with development of a consensus by the full group.

9. Whether the Implementation Plan or some other tool is used to manage the Plan for Success process, quarterly planning and Review & Reload sessions are essential to keeping strategic planning an ongoing, productive process and not a one-time event.

10. Recall the maxim 'Plans are worthless, but planning is everything.' Dedicate uninterrupted, meaningful time to the planning initiative to avoid redesigning the airplane while you are trying to fly it.

Citations and References

Part II – Strategy

1. For more information on famous and inspirational quotes see BrainyQuote, https://www.brainyquote.com/; Quote Investigator, https://quoteinvestigator.com/.

2. Alan Lakein, *How to Get Control of Your Time and Your Life* (New York: Signet, 1989).

3. For additional information on Dwight Eisenhower's quote see Garson O'Toole, "Plans are Worthless, but Planning is Everything," Quote Investigator®, November 18, 2017, https://quoteinvestigator.com/2017/11/18/planning/.

4. Adam Hayes, "Management by Objectives (MBO): Learn Its 5 Steps, Pros and Cons," Investopedia, updated August 30, 2022, https://www.investopedia.com/terms/m/management-by-objectives.asp.

5. See Will Kenton, "What Is Strategic Management?," Investopedia, updated October 2, 2022, https://www.investopedia.com/terms/s/strategic-management.asp.

6. For additional information of Mission (and Vision) statements see Comparably, Inc.(website), https://www.comparably.com/; Mission Statement Academy (website), https://mission-statement.com/.

7. Patrick Lencioni, *The Advantage: Why Organizational Health Trumps Everything Else in Business* (San Francisco: Jossey-Bass, 2012).

8. For more on the quote from Peter Drucker, see Garson O'Toole, "Efficiency is Concerned with Doing Things Right. Effectiveness is Doing the Right Things," Quote Investigator®, April 9, 2021, https://quoteinvestigator.com/2021/04/09/doing-right/.

9. See Ross Pounds, "The Roles and Responsibilities of a Board of Directors," Diligent Corporation, May 4, 2022, https://www.diligent.com/insights/board-of-directors/the-roles-and-responsibilities-of-a-board-of-directors/; also see Belle Wong, J.D., "Roles and Duties of Your Board of Directors," LegalZoom.com, Inc., updated January 6, 2023, https://www.legalzoom.com/articles/role-and-duties-of-your-board-of-directors; Tim Vire, "What Is a Board of Directors, Its Structure, Roles, and Responsibilities," OnBoard, Passageways, February 11, 2022, https://www.onboardmeetings.com/blog/board-director-structure-roles-responsibilities/.

10. Dennis Gabor, *Inventing the Future* (London: Secker & Warburg, 1963).

11. Harvey Schachter, "How Great Leaders Know the Right Questions to Ask," *The Globe and Mail*, Monday January 26, 2014, Morning Manager, https://www.theglobe-andmail.com/report-on-business/careers/management/how-to-ask-the-right-questions/article16458367/.

12. See Peter Fisk, "Question Burst," Peter Fisk's official website, January 18, 2020, https://www.peterfisk.com/2020/01/question-burst.

13. See Dan Oswald, "Asking the Right Questions is Key to Finding the Right Answers," HR Daily Advisor, Business and Learning Resources (BLR), a division of Simplify Compliance, LLC, updated January 7, 2018, https://hrdailyadvisor.blr.com/2015/03/30/asking-the-right-questions-is-key-to-finding-the-right-answers/.

14. Kaihan Krippendorff, "4 Steps to Breakthrough Ideas," Fast Company, September 6, 2012, https://www.fastcompany.com/3001044/4-steps-breakthrough-ideas.

15. Hal Gregersen, *Questions are the Answer: A Breakthrough Approach to Your Most Vexing Problems* (New York: Harper-Business, 2018).

16. Leo Tilman and Charles Jacoby, *Agility: How to Navigate the Unknown and Seize Opportunity in a World of Disruption* (Arlington, VA: Missionday, 2019).

17. See George T. Doran, "There's a S.M.A.R.T. Way to Write Management's Goals and Objectives," Department of Management Information Systems, Temple University Fox School of Business, November 1981, https://community.mis.temple.edu/mis0855002fall2015/files/2015/10/S.M.A.R.T-Way-Management-Review.pdf.

18. For additional information on closed loop communication, see Jarie Bolander, "6 Steps to Closed-Loop Communications," *The Daily MBA* (blog), July 31, 2019, https://www.thedailymba.com/2019/07/31/6-steps-to-closing-the-loop/.

Additional Resources

In addition to the specific sources outlined above, internet searches on the following topical headings will provide a wealth of additional information and insights on the topics discussed in Part II:

- Strategy in business
- Strategic planning
- Strategic planning process (models)
- Management by Objective
- Strategic management
- SWOT Analysis
- North Star in business
- Thematic goals

Part III

EXECUTION

Chapter 11

AN INTRODUCTION
TO *EXECUTION*

George Patton has been quoted saying, "A good plan, violently executed now, is better than a perfect plan next week." This could be interpreted with an emphasis on the quality of the plan. That is, comparing a "good" plan to a "perfect" plan. This frame of reference aligns with the observation of the great thinker Voltaire that "best is the enemy of the good" or Winston Churchill's quip that "perfection is the enemy of progress."[1] In either instance, the emphasis is on avoiding delay in execution while waiting for a more perfect plan. An alternative viewpoint shifts the emphasis to execution, wherein violent execution is a greater determinant of success than the quality of the plan. This was likely Patton's perspective relative to his military operations!

In the context of our recipe, business success is far more likely to occur when a relevant plan (Strategy) is aggressively implemented (Execution) by a fully engaged workforce (Culture). With this paradigm, perfection is not necessary. Instead, the plan, or more precisely the Strategy, must be relevant to achieving the organization's thoughtful goals. And success is more likely when the workforce is fully engaged, or more precisely, the Culture is fully aligned with the organization's Strategy. What remains, in perhaps less dramatic terms than those used by Patton when describing military circumstances, is *aggressive execution*.

Recalling the metaphor from the introduction to Part I in chapter 1, strategy is depicted as the front wheel, fork, and handlebars of a bike. It is used to set direction for where the organization is headed and make necessary course corrections. Culture is depicted as the chain, cogs, and back wheel. Culture provides the drive train to move the organization forward. But without a rider, the bike doesn't move. Alternatively, without execution, the best-laid strategy will never be implemented, and the benefits of an aligned culture will never be realized.

As illustrated in Figure 11.1 below, Culture, Strategy, and Execution are parts of an integrated system. They must work together in unison to achieve desired outcomes. Business strategy must be built upon an organization's culture, and organizational culture must be aligned with and supportive of the business' strategy. But nothing happens without execution. The better the execution, the greater the likelihood of success. And Success (*conducting a lawful, ethical, profitable, and sustainable business to grow value for stakeholders over the long term while embracing social, environmental, and governance responsibilities*) is what we are striving for. It is the ultimate purpose for and destination of our journey.

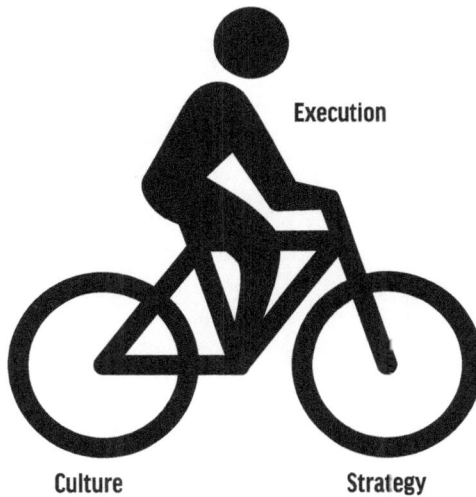

Figure 11.1: Three parts of an integrated system acting in unison

In chapter 12 we will explore 3 prerequisites to efficient and effective execution. In chapters 13 and 14 we will explore critical keys to organizational Culture and effectively implementing and maintaining the business Strategy as defined during Parts I and II, respectively. And in the Epilogue to follow, we will describe steps necessary to ensure that Culture, Strategy, and Execution are not seen as independent variables, but where each has a role to play in and are essential ingredients to our Recipe for Business Success. We will also emphasize the need for frequent monitoring, review, and revision of our recipe to ensure it remains effective and relevant as circumstances change.

Chapter 12

PREREQUISITES TO EFFICIENT AND EFFECTIVE *EXECUTION*

E fficient execution requires working in a well-organized and competent way to achieve maximum productivity with minimum wasted effort or expense. Effective execution requires focus on specifically desired goals and intended results. The strategy-aligned Core Ideology resulting from the assessment processes outlined in Part I creates a verbal picture of a compelling, desired future state of organizational culture. The Strategy resulting from the planning processes outlined in Part II defines in broad terms the intended goals and marshals the required resources (people, time, money) to accomplish those goals. In both instances, aggressive Execution of the resulting plans is required to take the organization from where it is today to where it should be in the future.

However, there are prerequisites to efficient and effective Execution of both Culture and Strategic plans. While others may emerge, the three key prerequisites include:

1. Establishing a positive culture of accountability,
2. Aligning leadership practices with the intended Culture and Strategy, and
3. Embracing lifelong learning to remain agile and open-minded during an era of exponential rate of change.

Accountability

Denotation is what a word literally means, whereas connotation describes the feelings the word evokes; the positive and negative associations that words frequently carry with them. Let's consider the word "accountable." Merriam-Webster[2] provides the literal definition or denotation as:

Definition of accountable
:   subject to giving an account
:   answerable

Wherein,
An account is further defined as
:   a statement explaining one's conduct
:   a statement or exposition of reasons, causes, or motives
And answerable is further defined as
:   liable to be called to account; responsible

The denotation, or literal meaning of the word "accountable," suggests being *subject to* and *answerable for* one's conduct, including an explanation of the reasons, causes, or motives. It should not come as a surprise that the connotation, or feelings the word *accountable* evokes, are described as unpleasant experiences involving blame, coercion, criticism, and more work.[3] The word *accountable* often connotes punishment or negative consequences. And while poor performance should not be tolerated and must be corrected, the first prerequisite for efficient and effective Execution of Culture and Strategy is to establish a positive culture of accountability. There are two suggested steps. The first step involves changing the paradigm associated with accountability and the second step involves creating clarity and focus on expectations.

Step 1 – Changing the Paradigm

The aspiration for a positive culture of accountability will not be fully realized without changing the traditional paradigm of accountability. The denotation (literal meaning) of the word *accountability* (in contrast to *accountable*) includes: an obligation **or willingness to accept** responsibility or to account for one's actions.[2] In this instance, accountability allows for the possibility for *willingness* to account for one's actions which may not carry as strong a negative connotation but is still not an affirmative or positive obligation to 'own' the outcome. This is where the paradigm must shift.

A positive attitude of accountability lies at the core of any effort to improve quality, satisfy clients, empower people, build teams, create new products, maximize effectiveness, and get results. Roger Connors and Tom Smith, authors of *Change the Culture – Change the Game* that we referenced in chapter 4, teamed with Craig Hickman to write *The*

Oz Principle – Getting Results Through Individual and Organizational Accountability.[4] *In* the Oz Principle, accountability is defined as:

> *A personal choice to rise above one's circumstances and demon-strate the ownership necessary for achieving desired results – to See It, Own It, Solve It, and Do It.*

The authors suggest that a thin line often separates success from failure. When we use excuses we abandon the opportunity to rise above ourselves, our circumstances, and our limitations. If we choose to continue feeling victimized, we will move through predictable stages in an unending 'below-the-line' cycle that thwarts individual and organizational productivity:

1. Ignoring or pretending not to know about my accountability;
2. Claiming it's not my job, ducking responsibility;
3. Blaming others for my predicament;
4. Citing confusion as an excuse for inaction, asking others to tell me what to do;
5. Claiming that I can't do it, developing my story for why I am not at fault, and finally
6. Waiting to see if some hoped-for miracle will be bestowed on me by an imaginary wizard.

When 'below-the-line,' individuals and teams fall into this blame game of excuses and rationalizations. Perhaps that might be expected given that the connotation of *accountable* has been described as unpleas-ant experiences involving blame, coercion, criticism, and more work.

'Above-the-line' behaviors require climbing what the authors suggest are the steps to accountability, including:

Recognizing reality @ See It
Asking "What else can I do" @ Own It
Inviting feedback @ Solve It
Taking action & accepting risk @ Do It

In a positive culture of accountability, people make personal choices to rise above their individual circumstances (i.e., no excuses or rationalizations) and take ownership necessary to achieve goals. When things go sideways and 'off plan' individuals recognize the reality without pointing fingers (i.e., See It), ask what else they can do to achieve mutually agreed upon results (i.e., Own It), invite feedback on their plans and performance (i.e., Solve It) and accept risks necessary to act and effect change (i.e., Do It).

Similarly, teams must act as a group of individuals who are collectively responsible for achieving objectives of the organization. In both instances, managers call attention to below-the-line behaviors and direct and reward people for making conscious choices to rise above their personal circumstances and demonstrate the type of ownership necessary for achieving the desired results, i.e., to See It, Own It, Solve It, and Do It. To do this in our recipe, people must have *Clarity and Focus* on those desired outcomes.

Step 2 – Creating Clarity and Focus

At the risk of offending some, most of us are ordinary people. To get extraordinary results from ordinary people there must be clarity in the work environment and focused attention on what matters most.

Answers must be readily apparent for typical questions like *what do I need to focus on, why is what I'm doing important, how does what I do fit into the big picture,* and *what does success look like?* All managers need to establish and maintain clarity with the people they lead and continually focus attention on those few things that really matter.

A process for establishing and maintaining *Clarity and Focus* with respect to organizational strategy was outlined in the Plan for Success component of the strategic planning model described in chapter 8. The process addressed 'focus' by establishing the short-term Key Strategic Initiatives for the year that are designed to achieve long-term goals. Definitions of Success created 'clarity' for each key strategy. All involved know exactly what success looks like. And with the Review and Reload process, the connection between the tasks on the 90-day Implementation Plan and the 'big picture' became readily apparent. Additional details on *Executing on Strategy* will be addressed in chapter 14. For now, it is enough to say that the Plan for Success component of the strategic planning model can be used as an example for creating clarity and focus on Strategy.

These same concepts, if not the same or similar tools (e.g., Implementation Plan) can be adopted for any team project. For instance, any workplace team could create a Plan for Success for their project. In this instance, project objectives and associated definitions of success would be created. The Implementation Plan or other project management tool might be used to break the project objectives down into bite-sized tasks. And a periodic Review & Reload session with After-Action Review questions might be used to monitor progress, promote accountability, and allow for course corrections. Utilizing a similar process to that used in strategic planning not only promotes a comparable level of clarity and focus among a project team but promotes efficiency by using effective business processes for multiple purposes.

And as will be described in greater detail in chapter 13 *Executing on Culture*, a similar process can be deployed to create clarity and focus on an individual basis. In summary, it involves asking each employee or category of worker to describe the Top 6 things they do, should do, or would like to do (within the context of their job description) to contribute to the organization's success. Serious debate should follow if there is a wide difference between the employee's desires and the needs of the organization.

It is the role of a leader to counsel the employee, identify their true needs (not wants), and close the gap on respective expectations. Once agreement is reached between individual and supervisor on the label and description of the Top 6 Roles, the individual can repeat the iterative process with their supervisor to reach mutually agreeable Definitions of Success for the year for each role. And when combined with a monthly 1:1 coaching session, *Clarity and Focus* is almost guaranteed. As indicated, this process is explored in much greater detail in chapter 13.

Establishing a positive culture of accountability at organizational, team, and individual levels is the first prerequisite for efficient and effective Execution. The next prerequisite involves aligning leadership style with the intended organizational Culture and Strategy.

Leadership

To be clear, even partially addressing the topic of leadership is well beyond the scope of this effort. Instead, we want to narrowly focus on how leadership, and specifically leadership style, should be supportive of business strategy and aligned with the intended culture.

There are numerous definitions of leadership. A common theme revolves around the skill of influencing people to act toward achieving goals in the common good. There are also numerous leadership styles characterized by the behaviors the leader manifests when influencing, guiding, and directing the work of the teams they lead. A short listing of some common leadership styles includes:

Affirmative	Delegative
Authoritative	Democratic
Autocratic	Laissez-faire
Bureaucratic	Pace-setting
Charismatic	Participative
Coaching	Transactional
Collaborative	Transformational

Each of these adjectives refer to one or more of the personalities of a leader. Knowing which leadership style lends itself to an individual's personality can improve a leader's ability to influence the behaviors of others. There are assessment tools that can be used to promote self-awareness, identify strengths, mitigate weaknesses, and develop as a leader. Some of the more frequently cited tools include:[5]

1. DISC Assessments
2. Meyers-Briggs Type Indicator®
3. USC's Interactive Leadership Style Assessment
4. CliftonStrengths and Gallup Strengthfinder
5. Emotional Intelligence (EQ) Assessments

However, as a prerequisite to efficient and effective Execution, our concern is narrowly focused on ensuring leadership practices align with the intended Culture and Strategy. Consider the denotation (literal meaning) of the common leadership styles listed:

- Affirmative - people come first, encourages cooperation and agreement within teams
- Authoritative – provides high-level direction, leads by example, uses personal vision to drive strategy and encourages team members to use their strengths
- Autocratic - command-and-control, do as I say, highly opinionated
- Bureaucratic – favors rigid structure to enact efficient systems and predictable outcomes
- Charismatic – uses exceptional communication skills, persuasiveness, and charm to influence behavior and connect with people
- Coaching – believes everyone has potential to develop their own strengths, guides work to achieve objectives
- Collaborative – breaks down silos, shares information and decision-making
- Delegative – creates the big picture and empowers individuals to exercise autonomy to achieve desired results
- Democratic – welcomes diverse input and perspective, encourages staff to exercise initiative and authority
- Laissez-faire - allows team members to take responsibility and make decisions
- Pace-setting – sets quick and fast pace, drives quick results, sink or swim

- Participative – engages in active listening, seeks innovative ideas, inclusive but not democratic decision-making
- Transactional – straightforward, sets goals for job at hand - promises and provides reward after completing tasks, or consequence if goals aren't met
- Transformational – inspires change and innovation; achieves goals through open lines of communication, demonstrating personal integrity and respect for staff's experience and knowledge

It is generally recognized that the there is no 'one size fits all' approach to leadership and that the style one is naturally inclined to employ is not appropriate for every situation. In fact, there are likely circumstances where each of the referenced styles may be both appropriate and effective. But what are the connotations or likely feelings associated with each style; the positive and negative associations that each style likely carries with it? The point is not to pass judgement on any leadership style. Rather, we want to explore how leadership style relates to the ability to align with the desired Culture and accomplish the stated Strategy.

Leadership style relates to the ability to align with the desired Culture and accomplish the stated Strategy.

In chapter 4 we provided ten examples of cultural orientation aligned with business strategy. The common attribute of all the examples was that the business strategy was built upon the organization's culture, and the organization's culture was aligned with and supportive of its business strategy. Our second prerequisite to efficient and effective Execution suggests that leadership style must also be aligned with Culture and Strategy. Building upon a few of the examples from chapter 4:

- We suggested that a strategically aligned culture for a manufacturer promising Zero Defects might be characterized as a Stable or Control culture. Such a culture would likely embrace a formalized, structured, and bureaucratic workplace, with detailed procedures directing what people do, but empowering workers to take all necessary in-process steps to avoid defects. An *authoritative* leadership style that provides high-level direction, leads by example, and encourages team members to contribute to Zero Defects could be appropriate. A *laissez-faire* leadership style that allows team members to define their own responsibilities and make independent decisions would likely be inconsistent with the desired Stable or Control culture.

- We suggested that a strategically aligned culture for a startup involved with autonomously operated vehicles might be characterized as a Creative or Innovative culture. Such a culture would likely embrace flexibility and adaptability, experimenting with new solutions, and individual initiative and freedom, with little emphasis on hierarchy. A *transformational* leadership style that inspires change and innovation, achieves goals through open lines of communication, and demonstrates personal integrity and respect for staff's experience and knowledge could be appropriate. A *bureaucratic* style that favors rigid structure to enact efficient systems and predictable outcomes would likely be inconsistent with a Create and Innovate culture.

- We suggested a strategically aligned culture for a company promoting high-return personal financial planning might be characterized as an Expertise or Results-Oriented culture. Such a culture would embrace figures and numbers being put on the table every time there is a discussion, and managers responsible for success using systems that reward employees based upon their achievements. A *transactional* leadership style that is straightforward and sets goals for the job-at-hand (promises and provides rewards after completing tasks, or consequences if goals aren't met) could be appropriate. A *charismatic* leader that uses exceptional communication skills, persuasiveness, and charm to influence behavior and connect with people would likely be inconsistent with an Expertise or Results-Oriented culture.

- We suggested a strategically aligned culture for charitable associations seeking a world without a specified disease or social ill might be characterized as an Authentic or Collaborative culture. Such a culture would likely embrace stakeholders connecting and working together for the benefit of humanity, conveying a desire to lift the human spirit to achieve their lofty aspirations. An *affirmative*, people-come-first leadership style that encourages cooperation and agreement, could be appropriate. An *autocratic*, command-and-control, do as I say leadership style would likely be inconsistent with an Authentic or Collaborative culture.

As described above, every manager has emotional intelligence and an underlying personality that support a preferred leadership style. However, good managers, while staying true to a central style, adapt their leadership preference to meet the needs of the specific circumstances and the organizational culture in general. This process should not be left to chance. *Intentional servant leadership* provides an excellent framework for engaging the specific styles of leadership necessary to accomplish strategic goals in alignment with organizational culture.

INTENTIONAL SERVANT LEADERSHIP

Servant leadership is likely noticeable by its absence in the discussion thus far. Servant leadership has gained great popularity since first being introduced by Robert Greenleaf in 1970 in his essay *The Servant as Leader*.[6] A servant leader is someone who identifies and meets the legitimate needs of their people, removes all the barriers to their success, so they can serve their customers. Servant leadership does not expect any outcome or reward other than simply fulling the needs of people. For our purposes in the Recipe for Business Success, servant leadership may be the most effective overall leadership strategy because the leader can adopt aspects of any of the common leadership styles outlined above to meet the needs of those they serve as circumstances warrant. That is, the servant leader can at times be authoritative, collaborative, or delegatory to meet the specific needs of the people they serve. These choices, however, must be intentional, and specifically selected to support the defined Strategy and in alignment with the desired Culture.

As described, intentional servant leadership must be consistently seen as the overall leadership strategy – a framework for defining and selecting techniques to respond to organizational needs. Intentional leaders define their desired outcomes, both stated and unstated, and anticipate the consequences of their actions, both intended and unintended. Servant leaders make a conscious choice to lead through service to others. Servant leaders identify the legitimate needs of their teams and remove barriers so others can be successful. When combined, the role of an intentional servant leader is to help ordinary people achieve extraordinary results. Adopting an intentional servant leadership strategy easily facilitates fulfillment of the second prerequisite of aligning leadership practices with the intended Culture and Strategy.

Lifelong Learning

By our definition, both cultural and strategic planning are ongoing, never-ending processes. This requires constant vigilance in monitoring both internal organizational health and the external business environment. Each change in the workforce, each introduction of new technology, each shift in macro- and micro- economics, geopolitics and the marketplace, demands your consideration. The third prerequisite to sustaining efficient and effective Execution requires leadership to embrace lifelong learning to remain agile and open-minded during an era of exponential rate of change. Each of these three attributes are described below.

EXPONENTIAL RATE OF CHANGE

Scientists, economists, futurists, and others have asserted that we have entered the fourth industrial revolution (IR4). The beliefs are that IR4 is being driven by a convergence of technology (e.g., artificial intelligence, gene editing, augmented reality, etc.), connectivity (e.g., quantum computing, internet-of-things, 5G broadband, etc.), and automation (e.g., autonomous vehicles, advanced robotics, smart factories, etc.), resulting in an exponential rate of change (an increase based on a constant multiplicative rate of change over equal increments of time). This phenomenon has placed increased demands on organizational agility.

AGILITY

IR4 necessitates increased attention to business agility. There are numerous definitions of business agility. Leo Tilman and General Charles Jacoby offer a detailed definition in their book *Agility – How to Navigate the Unknown and Seize Opportunity in a World of Disruption.*[7]

> The organizational capacity to effectively detect, assess, and respond to environmental changes in ways that are purposeful, decisive, and grounded in the will to win.

This definition recognizes the need to first detect, then assess, and ultimately respond to changes in the environment, and suggests the response must be purposeful, decisive, and grounded in a will to win. However, to be agile one must be open to change.

OPEN-MINDEDNESS (AND INTELLECTUAL HUMILITY)

Shane Snow, in his text *Dream Teams – Working Together Without Falling Apart*,[8] describes the traits of teams that change the course of history – that transform industries, break cycles of oppression or stagnation, or win consecutive championships. Open-mindedness and intellectual humility are among these traits. Open-mindedness means being critically receptive to alternative possibilities. Being willing to think again despite having formed an opinion, and sincerely trying to avoid those conditions and offset those factors which constrain and distort our reflections. Intellectual humility (IH) is a non-threatening awareness of one's intellectual fallibility. It is being willing to change our viewpoint without freaking out. An intellectually humble person finds the right balance between dogmatically rejecting the dissenting viewpoints of others and yielding too quickly in the face of intellectual conflict. Those high in IH demonstrate openness to revising one's important opinions, are less likely to demonize others for changing their attitudes, and are better able to detect the validity of persuasive arguments. Intellectual humility isn't just the ability to change. It makes one more likely to correctly judge when it's time to change.

Some suggest 'deep immersion' through job rotation, intense formal education, and lengthy travel assignments (especially in foreign countries) offer effective ways to gain the open-mindedness and IH necessary to create an agile organization (as defined above) in the environment of IR4. However, few leaders have the luxury of such 'offline' investments of resources (people, time, money). Reading, coupled with experiential learning (i.e., application of learned skills) is an effective alternative that helps develop the desired (and aligned) leadership practice.

Developing Your Leadership Practice

We have all heard and perhaps even used the expression of 'medical practice' or 'legal practice,' or even 'yoga practice.' In these instances, "practice" suggests the actual application of and use of methods or skills, as opposed to theories relating to them. But how many intentionally consider their "Leadership Practice" and intentionally incorporate habitual exercises to maintain and improve one's proficiency as a leader?

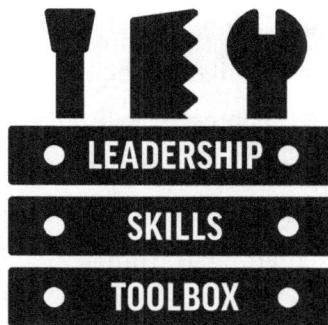

Figure 12.1: Building a leadership skills toolbox

Consider your inventory of available leadership skills as a toolbox. What is the depth and breadth of the skills available for your use to execute on culture and strategic plans efficiently and effectively? Or to detect, assess, and respond to rapidly changing environments with purpose and decisiveness? Reading and associated experiential learning should be intentionally designed to help develop your leadership practice. Book clubs among members of a leadership team, in conjunction with formal debates of controversial topics (see referenced rules for debates)[9] and real-world application of skills, are examples of the type of experiential lifelong learning necessary to remain agile and open-minded during an era of exponential rate of change. Selections from the *Citations and References* listed in the final chapter to each Part of this Recipe for Business Success might be a good place to start.

Summary

We established three essential ingredients for our Recipe for Business Success: Culture, Strategy, and Execution. There are prerequisites for a chef working to prepare a fabulous meal. Likewise, there are prerequisites necessary to prepare for exceptional Execution in business. Efficient and effective *Executing on Culture* as described in chapter 13 will not occur without intentional alignment of leadership style with the desired culture. Similarly, efficient and effective *Executing on Strategy* as described in chapter 14 will not occur without a positive culture of accountability. And efficient and effective Execution of both the Culture and Strategy plans will only be sustainable when leadership embraces lifelong learning and development of their leadership practice.

Within our Recipe for Business Success, the prerequisites to exceptional Execution of both Culture and Strategic plans include:

- Establishing a positive culture of accountability,
- Aligning leadership practices with the intended Culture and Strategy, and
- Embracing lifelong learning to remain agile and open-minded during an era of exponential rate of change.

With these prerequisites in place, the chef can prepare for fabulous *Success*.

Chapter 13

EXECUTING ON CULTURE

Management trends come and go. Economic conditions fluctuate and market demands shift. Corporations restructure and new owners take over. The one constant, the one enduring truth, is that people, starting with the senior executive, define the character of a company. They always have and always will. Motivated, passionate people make the difference between ho-hum mediocrity and extraordinary performance. That's the message from Peter W. Schutz, former CEO of Porsche AG and author of *The Driving Force*.[10] Schutz asserts that people are the heart and soul of any business. Many businesses suggest that "our people are our greatest asset." But how many go about intentionally recruiting and developing their greatest asset around their desired culture?

In chapter 2 we presented three elements to an organization's core ideology, including:

- Core Purpose – describing **Why** *we exist*; our *noble cause*

- Cultural Beliefs and Values - describing **How** *we behave*
- Mission - describing **What** *we do*

In chapter 3 we explored techniques to assess each of these attributes as they exist today and create a vision of where the culture might aspire. And in chapter 4 we explored how to progress from where today's culture is to the aspirational culture of the future. It included a 7-step process to implement and maintain the desired culture, built upon a framework of human behavior and neuropsychology. But even when successful, with each new generation that enters the workforce, each new hire, transfer, or promotion, and each change in technology introduced into the workplace, behaviors and interactions take on new patterns that eventually result in new cultural norms. The key to *Executing on Culture* is to continually focus on people, and specifically the role culture plays in recruiting and developing talent in a positive culture of accountability. To paraphrase Jim Collins, author of *Built to Last* and *Good to Great*, our human systems must work to get the right people onto the bus (and the wrong people off), in seats that maximize individual contributions, while working together with their peers in pursuit of the common good of the organization.[11]

Organizations that truly believe their people are their greatest asset intentionally act on that belief. They adopt human systems best practices relative to recruiting, selection, and onboarding new talent. They establish professional development, performance management, and succession planning best practices to retain and grow the depth and breadth of their talent throughout their careers. There are articles, books, seminars, and courses, if not entire degree programs and professional associations, that address the range of desired human systems best practices. Naturally, this is well beyond the scope of our Recipe for Business Success. As indicated above, the key to *Executing on Culture* is to focus specifically on the role culture plays in recruiting and developing talent in a positive culture of accountability.

While we will not be doing a deep dive into the breadth of human systems best practices, the importance of tightly interweaving them with the strategic plan must be emphasized. Strategic initiatives must drive the entire recruiting and talent management processes. Long-term development plans for existing staff must reflect their individual talents and desires but must also be shaped by the intended direction of the organization – i.e., enterprise, business unit, or product or service line team. Human systems must embrace desired cultural beliefs and values. In fact, every element of human systems must not only be in alignment with those beliefs but must also actively demonstrate them.

Actions speak louder than words. Every action along the life of employment continuum as illustrated below should be fundamentally rooted in the desired cultural beliefs and values (i.e., the outcomes of chapter 3). For purposes of our discussion, the course of employment can be broken down into a recruiting phase where talent is brought onto the team, and a talent management phase where talent is nurtured and developed.

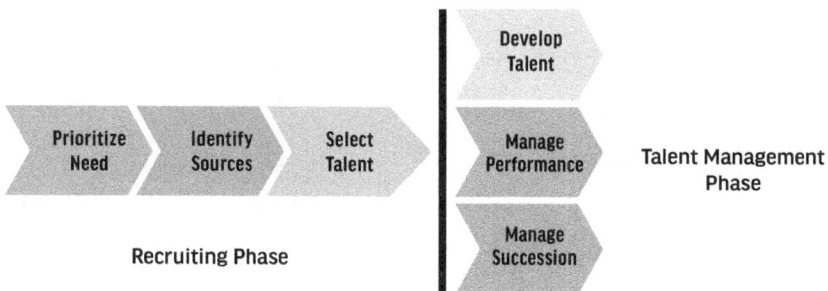

Figure 13.1: Employment continuum

The three elements of the Recruiting phase outlined above are sequential. A team identifies, defines and prioritizes needs, establishes a recruiting strategy to get qualified candidates into the selection funnel, and then implements a process to screen, interview and select top talent. Within the context of *Executing on Culture*, we will limit our discussion to use of cultural assessments and cultural interviewing as part of the talent selection process.

The three elements of the Talent Management phase; professional development, performance management, and succession management, are concurrent and each must be continually addressed over the lifetime of employment. Within the context of *Executing on Culture*, we will limit our discussion to promotion of a positive culture of accountability and adoption of desired cultural norms as part of an integrated performance management process.

The Recruiting Phase – Use of cultural assessments and cultural interviewing

As described by Travis Bradberry & Jean Graves in their book *Emotional Intelligence 2.0*,[12] there are three components of every person that factor into their likely success at a given job. These include:

- Cognitive Capability – generally measured by Intelligence Quotient (IQ), but more broadly defined as Knowledge, Skills, and Attributes.
- Emotional Intelligence – generally measured by Emotional Quotient (EQ), representing one's ability to recognize and understand emotions in oneself and others, and one's ability to use this awareness to manage behavior and relationships.

- Personality Type – generally measured as behavioral traits that represent the "style" that defines each of us, such as a preference towards introversion or extroversion

The question isn't simply, *Does the candidate possess certain core competencies?* The more difficult and more important question is, Can the candidate's core competencies be brought to bear in the specific situational fit of the organization's work environment?

Can the candidate's core competencies be brought to bear in the specific situational fit of the organization's work environment?

Situational fit relates to the candidates meshing with the organization's environment, intensity, cultural beliefs and values, and mission. Organizations that have completed the exercises described in Part I have the advantage of being able to articulate the work environment and core ideology that underpin it. The key is to uncover alignment issues during the interviewing process. From a testing perspective, this is best approximated by EQ, although some overlap with behavioral or personality traits come into play. Note, it is arguable that personal assessment surveys of any form should not be used to make hiring decisions (i.e., a strict Go/No Go decision). Instead, they should be considered to help inform the interviewing process (as will be described below). With this caveat in mind, background on EQ and personality type assessments is offered.

Emotional Intelligence Assessments

Emotional Intelligence is your ability to recognize and understand emotions in yourself and others, and your ability to use this awareness to manage your behavior and engage in relationships. Emotional intelligence is a fundamental element of human behavior that is distinct from intellect (IQ) and is measured by one's Emotional Quotient (EQ) or Emotional Intelligence (EI).[12] There are several well recognized and researched testing methodologies to assess EQ. There are common attributes among all of them. Broadly, they test in two overarching areas of Personal Competence (comprised of Self Awareness and Self-Management), and Social Competence (comprised of Social Awareness and Relationship Management). Some methodologies add a third overarching category of Optimism. These broad areas may be broken down further into specific attributes like self-regard or interpersonal relationships. Examples of EQ/EI assessments include:

- The Emotional Quotient Inventory 2.0 (EQ-i-2.0)
- Profile of Emotional Competence (PEC)
- The Trait Emotional Intelligence Questionnaire (TEIQue)
- Wong's Emotional Intelligence Scale (WEIS)
- The Emotional and Social Competence Inventory (ESCI)

Personality Trait Assessments

Along with IQ and EQ, Personality is the third and final piece of the puzzle when trying to size up the whole person using assessment tools. It is the "style" that defines each of us. Personality is the result of preferences or traits, such as an inclination to introversion or extroversion. Like IQ, personality cannot be used to predict EQ. Also like IQ, personality is stable over a lifetime. Personality traits appear early in life, and they generally do not shift except in response to life-changing events.[12] There are multiple assessments available to help define personality preferences or tendencies. Two of the most popular assessments – Meyers-Briggs Type Indicator (MBTI)® and DISC – are described below.

Meyers-Briggs Type Indicator® (MBTI)

The MBTI is designed to illustrate the way one thinks and deals with information, including the conscious and unconscious forces affecting behaviors. It is designed to identify a relative position along a spectrum of four *bipolar* dimensions of core personality traits that differentiate people.[13, 14] The four bipolar dimensions are described as follows.

1. Extroversion (E) vs Introversion (I): Individuals pay more attention to and get their energy from either the external world of objects and people (extroversion), or the inner world of ideas and feelings (introversion).

2. Sensing (S) vs Intuiting (N): Individuals naturally prefer to use one of two functions. Either sensing what the objective facts are (reality) or intuiting relationships and possibilities (imagination).

3. Thinking (T) vs Feeling (F): Individuals process and evaluate information one of two ways. Either by using logic and objectivity (thinking) or subjectively using personal values (feeling).

4. Judging (J) vs Perceiving (P): Individuals deal with the outside world in two different ways. Either you prefer structure and firm decisions (judging) or you prefer a world that's more open, flexible, and adaptable (perceiving).

The MBTI model assumes that while both facets of each bi-polar dimension are present in a personality, one is emphasized more than the other. In fact, an individual may use one consciously and with deliberate intention, while the other influences behavior only unconsciously.

DISC

DISC is an acronym describing four behavioral dimensions, as defined below. People describing DISC often start with what DISC is not. It is not a measurement of emotional intelligence, personal intelligence, motivation, or education and training. It's also not a measurement of one's experience, personal skills, or world view. What DISC does measure is **how** you do what you do. It is a measure of one's *observable* behavior.[15] Like MBTI, DISC is a neutral language. Meaning, there are no good or bad behavioral styles.

The four dimensions of behavioral style assessed in the DISC methodology include:

- **D**ecisive — your preference for problem solving and getting results
- **I**nteractive — your preference for interacting with others and showing emotion
- **S**tability — your preference for pacing, persistence, and steadiness
- **C**autious — your preference for procedures, standards, and protocols

Each of the DISC dimensions is scored on a continuum from 0 (Low) to 100 (High). Each dimension is scored based upon one's Natural

Style (how they behave when they are most natural), and Adaptive Style (how they behave when they are being observed or are consciously aware of their behavior).

Note that the online sources of organizational cultural assessment tools outlined in chapter 4 may also offer individual self-assessment tools that could be used in the candidate selection process. In addition, the previously referenced article posted on Journey to Leadership titled *Top 10 Leadership Assessment Tools for 2022* provides further insights.[5] Regardless, as indicated previously, assessment tools may play a role in assessing the situational fit of a candidate with respect to the work environment and culture, but they are best used to inform the questions to be explored during the actual interview process.

Cultural Interviewing

Cultural interview questions attempt to determine if there is a good fit between the organization's core ideology and the candidate's personal values, beliefs, and work ethic, and what the candidate might add to the existing culture. The emphasis is not on eliminating candidates, but rather finding those that share common values and will most likely contribute to success. The way a candidate answers culture fit interview questions reveals a lot about their preferred work style, their preferred type of work environment, and their personal beliefs and values.

The emphasis is not on eliminating candidates, but rather finding those that share common values and will most likely contribute to success.

A quick internet search under "Culture Interview Questions" results in no shortage of questions that could be asked. According to multiple sources, 10 common interview questions include:

- Describe the environment in which you work best.
- Describe your ideal boss or supervisor.
- Do you prefer to work alone or on a team?
- What motivates you?
- How important is work-life balance?
- How did you fit in with the culture while working with your current/last employer?
- How would your current/last coworkers describe you?
- What would the ideal company culture look like for you?
- Which of our core values resonates most with you?
- Why do you want to work for us?

There is nothing inherently wrong with these common questions, but efficient and effective Execution on Culture suggests that investing time and effort in tailoring questions to specifically explore the organization's stated core ideology may be warranted. In this manner, the group of questions selected would explore each element of the established cultural beliefs and values (as defined in Part I). For instance, if a cultural belief revolves around teamwork and a participative and collaborative work environment, questions like "Do you prefer to work alone or on a team?" or "Why do people like working with/for you?" take on greater relevance. Similarly, questions should be developed to explore each core and aspirational value and the associated behaviors that are expected in the workplace. For instance, if responding to customers in a timely and responsive manner is an expected behavior, a question might be "Tell me about a situation with a frustrated or disappointed customer and how you handled it."

The process for recording and the criteria for scoring responses to cultural interviewing questions should also be established dispassionately during the question development process and long before any actual interviews are conducted. To achieve a desirable outcome of good cultural fit, it is important that each interviewer ask similar questions and evaluates the responses using similar, previously agreed upon criteria.[16,17]

Of course, getting the right people onto the bus is only the first step. The goal is to continually deploy people to be of greatest value (i.e., in the best seat on the bus), working together for the common good of the organization. From a cultural alignment perspective, this requires a process for evaluating performance and developing talent that includes assessment of actual workplace behaviors and encourages a continual positive culture of accountability.

Talent Management Phase - Using performance management to drive results

Performance management should be the most important part of an employee's experience with an organization. It has the potential to be the link that ties everything together, including creating a positive culture of accountability and reinforcing desired behaviors. Performance management is the furthest thing from a disciplinary process; instead, it is the most effective way for an organization to bring its core ideology to life. Before we get too far into this topic it is important to explore some key concepts. Let's start with the traditional performance appraisal.[18,19]

Typically , for reasons illustrated on the sidebar, neither supervisor nor employee enjoys the experience. And the single biggest reason for its shortcoming is that there is little to no focus on comparison of mutually understood expectations and corresponding results.

Performance Appraisals Are:

1. Conducted too infrequently;
2. Largely impersonal and one-sided;
3. Frequently involve forced rankings, and are;
4. Routinely argumentative and seldom productive.

One of the biggest systemic problems existing within many organizations is the lack of clarity about goals. Employees may know what responsibilities are included in their job descriptions, but frequently lack a true understanding of the specific results to be achieved within any given period. How can they then be evaluated about their performance if it is not based on mutually accepted and quantifiable personal goals?

Consider a definition of *performance management* from the People & Culture team at UC Berkeley that, unlike performance appraisal, is supportive of a positive culture of accountability.[20]

An ongoing process of communication between a supervisor and an employee that occurs routinely throughout the year, in support of accomplishing mutually accepted and quantifiable personal goals that are in alignment with the strategic objectives of the organization.

The essential ingredient for a performance management system to work is to have goals which are not only mutually agreed upon and well defined but are also quantifiable. It's difficult to make yourself put a lot of energy into reaching a goal in which you are not personally invested. The key to success is for the goals to have an element of personal desire. The employee must take ownership of the goals and hold themselves accountable.

It's also of value to build on success by having short-term objectives that contribute towards longer-term goals. It should be noted that the 5-step process outlined in the sidebar as elements of a performance management system are similar to the

Elements of a Performance Management (PM) System:

1. Establishing Clarity and Focus
2. Annual Definitions of Success
3. 90-day Implementation Plan
4. Monthly 1:1 Meetings
5. Quarterly and Annual "After Action Reviews"

elements of the Plan for Success in strategic planning outlined in chapter 8 and when first introducing the concept of clarity and focus with respect to accountability in chapter 11. This is intentional. There is a degree of efficiency achieved when similar business processes can be adapted for multiple beneficial uses.

Establishing Clarity and Focus

Much has been written on the benefits of focusing on clarity to drive performance.[21,22] Each organization should adopt a process to establish clarity and focus for each individual (or group of individuals) in every role. Start by asking each employee (or category of worker) to reflect on their respective job description and answer the following question:

What are the six most important things you do, should do, or would like to do this year?

There is no single process to follow to answer this question, but brainstorming is usually a great place to start. Ask the employee to create a list of one- or two-word descriptions of what roles they take on to achieve success. The list should be as long as possible and should be developed over several days as the most important determinants to success are frequently the last to make it to the list. This process involves divergent thinking in that each employee is opening their eyes to the total range of possibilities. The next step is convergent thinking, where each employee is asked to narrow the range and focus on what is most important.

Now is the time to prioritize the elements on the list. The list may be long and include many things the employee does, but the task at hand is to identify the most important. Consider the 80/20 rule and ask "What are the 20 percent of activities that cause 80 percent of results?" This should result in answers to the central question outlined above, *"What are the six most important things you do, should do, or would like to do this year."* Note that if 'Our employees are our greatest asset,' one of those *most important things* we do should be *professional development.* For one of their Top 6 Roles, everyone should be a "Student" engaged in lifelong learning throughout their career. Therefore, the challenge just got more difficult as the range of possibilities needs to be distilled down to the other top 5 things we do, should do, or would like to do, in addition to the 6th role of being a Student (i.e., professional development).

Note that if 'Our employees are our greatest asset,' one of those *most important things* we do should be *professional development.*

Once the Top 6 Roles are listed (described in one or two words), it's time to add a description of the role. This is the next step in defining what success looks like. The description of the term should be concise (a short sentence) yet convey the individual's use of the term.

Once the employee has drafted their Top 6 Roles and associated one sentence descriptions, it's time to sit down with the supervisor. There must be total alignment on the Top 6 Roles and the associated descriptions. There can be no ambiguity. The Clarity and Focus document should be edited until a mutual understanding is achieved. Only then should you progress to defining what success looks like.

Definition of Success

A supervisor and employee must have a common understanding of the most important things the employee does, should do or wants to do in their role. Reaching agreement on the top roles for an employee is the first step necessary to achieve success. But this doesn't define what success looks like. The following questions should be considered when developing the Definitions of Success for each Top Role:

- What is the best use of my time right now?
- What is my role in achieving the organization's key strategic initiatives?
- What are the Critical Result Areas or Key Performance Indicators I contribute to?
- What commitments have I already made?
- What do I need to do now to develop professionally?

Mutually agreed upon clear and measurable goals must be established for each of the Top 6 Roles, each year. This can be captured in a simple document wherein you ask, "I will know I've been successful in 20XX when...:" For instance, let's assume for a moment that one of the Top 6 roles for a given position is "Group Leader" and the description of the term has been agreed upon. The complete definition of success statement would look like:

GROUP LEADER

As a Group Leader, I ensure decisions made, actions taken, and emotions created within my team are aligned with common goals; I identify and meet the needs of staff, and remove barriers to their success.

I will know I've been successful when, by xx/yy/zzzz, I have:
- *The first specific measure of success*
- *The second specific measure of success*
- *The third specific measure of success*
- *Etc.*

To be effective, the bulleted items must be **S**pecific (clear and under-standable to all parties), **M**easurable (there can be no debate on whether the goal has been achieved) and **A**chievable (in 12 months), **R**elevant to the role, and **T**imebound (by xx/yy/zzzz). These SMART goals define what success looks like *for the year*. The Implementation Plan (i.e., the same tool used in strategic planning) can be used as the tool to guide and monitor success.

The Implementation Plan

The best way to ensure each employee is successful is to establish clear expectations of what "success" looks like (Top 6 Roles and Definitions of Success), and then discuss progress on an ongoing basis. Effective use of the Implementation Plan involves four components.

1. Headlining Top 6 Roles

The top row of blocks contains a header to list the one- or two-word description for the Top 6 Roles determined in the Clarity and Focus exercise described above. The box immediately below the Header is used to describe the essential elements of the role in the header. As indicated previously, the Clarity and Focus document should be retained to reference the complete description of each role. For Implementation Plan purposes, a short-annotated version is adequate.

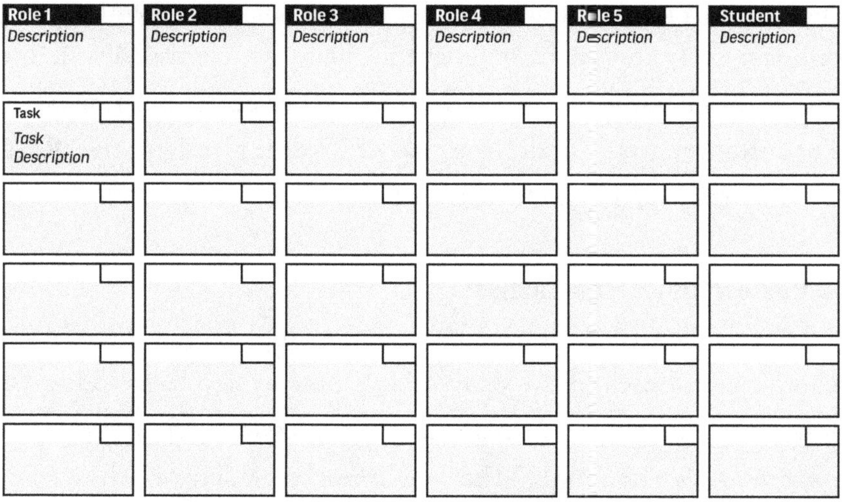

Figure 13.2: Personal implementation plan

It should be noted that one of the columns in the Implementation Plan already includes a header for the suggested universal role of "Student" and an associated description of "I foster continuous development and improvement in the knowledge and skills needed for career development and personal fulfilment."

2. Developing a Plan of Action

Each column contains 5 task cells that constitute the Plan of Action for a given quarter. For each column, 3 to 5 tasks that must be initiated and/or completed during the quarter are described. Accomplishing these tasks constitutes success. There should be at least 3 tasks, if not the Plan of Action probably lacks specificity (i.e., tasks are too broadly worded). To maintain focus there should never be more than 5 tasks.

Each task that is elected must be **S**pecific and **M**easurable. **S**pecific means that both the employee and the supervisor understand the task and can easily restate the objective in their own words. **M**easurable means they'll both know when the task is achieved; it's unambiguous. For instance, a task under the role of "Student" might say "Read *5 Dysfunctions of a Team* by Patrick Lencioni."

3. Review for Reasonableness

After the Plan of Action section of the Implementation Plan is completed for each of the six roles, it is time to step back and assess it for reasonableness. Remember the expression, *"If everything is important, then nothing is!"* The final litmus test is simple – the overall Plan of Action must be **A**chievable *in 90 days* – that is, all tasks must be completed or at a minimum, work must be initiated, in 90 days. If there is too much in the Plan of Action, it must be reduced. If the Plan of Action is not challenging enough, it must be expanded. If there are tasks that won't be started until the next quarter, move them to the "parking lot" for the next quarter. The final draft should be reviewed and negotiated with the supervisor. Now there is a mutually shared definition of success and the specific tasks necessary to get there.

4. Monitoring Progress

Begin preparing for a monthly 1:1 (described below) by color-coding the Implementation Plan to reflect the status of each/every task in the Plan of Action. By convention, if a task is listed in the Plan of Action, it is to be completed during the 90-day cycle, or work must have been initiated and be on schedule. With that as the overarching criteria, the following color codes are appropriate:

White – all planned work is done – the task is Complete. The task should be left on the Implementation Plan until a new Plan of Action is developed for the next quarter.

Green – the task is on schedule – we have Traction. It should remain on the Implementation Plan until Completed, including carrying over to the next quarter if/as needed.

Yellow – there is some wheel spin and some traction – we have Mixed results. Emphasis should be redirected to this task to create traction as quickly as possible.

Red – work is substantively behind schedule – we have Wheel Spin. A corrective action plan should be developed to correct the shortfall and regain traction.

Gray – work is not scheduled to begin yet – the task is Pending. Note that since work is to be initiated, if not completed, on every task in the Plan of Action within the respective quarter, then a task cannot be "Pending" for more than 2 months.

The Implementation Plan may be modified to include a block to assess alignment with the organization's Core Ideology similar to that illustrated below.

Alignment	Belief	Belief	Belief	Core Value	Core Value	Core Value	Core Value
NAME							
The Bar	+	+	+	+/-	+/-	+/-	+/-

Key:	
+	Exceptional Alignment
+/–	Mixed Result
–	Lacked Alignment

Figure 13.3: Core ideology assessment

The "score" for any *Belief* or *Value* is either +, +/-, or -. **The focus is on demonstrable action** since the previous meeting, and not whether or not the individual believes in the belief or value. A "+" means the individual has demonstrated exceptional alignment with a value by exemplifying one or more of the normative behaviors associated with that value. A "+/-" indicates a mixed result – a clearly demonstrable action doesn't jump out. A "–" indicates that a demonstrable action ran contrary to acceptable behavior. All minuses should be confronted during the 1:1 meeting described below.

1:1 Meetings

We adopted the definition of performance management earlier as *an ongoing process of communication between a supervisor and an employee that occurs routinely throughout the year,* in support of accomplishing mutually accepted and quantifiable personal goals that are in alignment with the strategic objectives of the company. It is recognized that not all employees will participate in

> **After each 1:1 Meeting it is important to review the Clarity & Focus form to make sure that the Implementation Plan and overall goals are aligned with the employee's Definition of Success.**

a 1:1 meeting with a supervisor or be required to complete Implementation Plans. However, there should be alternative methods of communicating performance expectations in place with all employees.

With completion of the Clarity and Focus exercise and development of a mutually agreed upon Implementation Plan as described above, nearly all elements of an effective performance management system have been established. All that remains is routine communication to monitor progress, resolve obstacles, and make course corrections as necessary as suggested in the Check-In: Providing Observation and Feedback portion of the previously cited UC Berkeley People & Culture guidance on performance management.[18] This requires an effective 1:1 meeting between supervisor and employee on a routine (minimum monthly) basis.

Consider the 1:1 as a private meeting between the Coach (supervisor) and a Player (employee). With our definition of performance management, however, the key to an effective 1:1 starts with the recognition that it is the Player's meeting. The Player sets the agenda and decides what is most important for him/her to discuss, while the Coach counsels and reserves the right to identify needed corrective behaviors. In addition to creating the report card by color-coding progress on the Implementation Plan, the Player should come to the meeting prepared to:

- Answer clarifying questions about issues of importance
- Be open to exploration of new concepts and approaches

Of course, it's not just the Player that needs to come prepared. The Coach needs to be prepared to:

- Asking clarifying questions to fully diagnose the Player's top issues
- Actively listen to what the Player is saying
- Show empathy to the challenges the Player is confronting
- Offer helpful input with concrete, specific suggestions

The effectiveness of any 1:1 meeting will be determined in large part by how deeply the Coach helps the Player explore top issues. Two techniques help to ensure effectiveness. The first deals with the Coach's ability to ask clarifying questions. A suggested process is illustrated below.

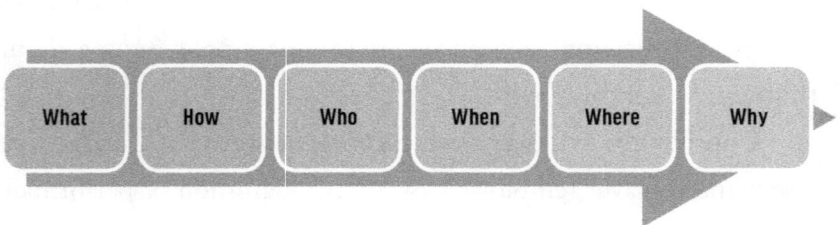

What	How	Who	When	Where	Why

Figure 13.4: Hierarchy of clarifying questions

There are a set of probing questions that help facilitate effective 1:1 meetings. The order of importance is illustrated in Fig. 13.4. The most important questions are "What" questions like "what are the obstacles, what have you tried to do to overcome them, what other ideas are you considering, etc.?" At the other end of the spectrum "Why" questions like "Why did you do that?" should be avoided. They can make the Player defensive even when asked with the best of intentions.

The second element to help ensure an effective 1:1 session deals with the structure of the conversation, as illustrated in Figure 13.5 below.

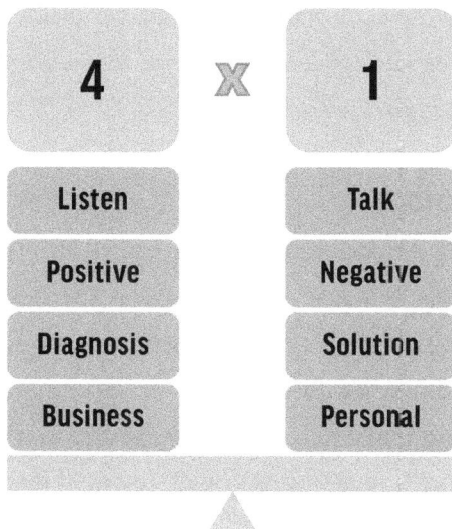

Figure 13.5: Effective 1:1 coaching skills

It is believed that if the Coach keeps to these 4:1 ratios the Player will perceive it to be "about equal." That is, keeping the 4:1 structure keeps the 1:1 session in "balance." The Coach needs to:

- Listen 4 times more than talk
- Explore/address positive aspects of issues 4 times more than negative aspects of the issue
- Ask diagnostic and clarifying questions 4 times more than offering solutions
- Address the business aspect of an issue 4 times more than the Player's personal involvement in the issue

To be considered effective, the outcome of any/every 1:1 session should be a plan co-created by the Player and the Coach, with mutual commitment to future review. The Coach should be cognizant of projects being worked on and obstacles uncovered during the 1:1. To achieve a positive culture of accountability, the Player must make *A personal choice to rise above one's circumstances and demonstrate the ownership necessary for achieving desired results — to See It, Own It, Solve It, and Do It.*

Course Corrections

Like the Review & Reload session of strategic planning, it is important to have a quarterly R&R session as part of the performance management system. This allows the manager and employee to monitor progress towards the annual Definitions of Success, promote personal accountability, and make necessary course corrections.

A simple process involves creating a consolidated workbook that contains a 'clarity and focus' form like illustrated in Figure 13.6, and tabs with Implementation Plans for each quarter. The 'clarity and focus' form outlines the Top 6 Roles, associated Descriptions, and annual Definitions of Success (as previously described). Four columns labeled Q1, Q2, Q3, Q4 are added with cells opposite each Definition of Success (DoS).

2021 Roles, Descriptions, and Definitions of Success			Status						
NAME - TITLE									
			Q1	Q2	Q3	Q4			
1. **Role:**									
Description: *As a \<Role>, I (ensure, implement, verify, oversee...)*									
Definition of Success: I will be considered successful in December 2023 when I									
•									
•									
•									
•									

Figure 13.6: Clarity and focus tool - role, description, definitions of success

During a quarterly R&R session, the employee self-assesses progress against each DoS by color coding the corresponding cell. As illustrated in the key in Figure 13.6, the color selection criteria is gray if still pending, green if on track, yellow for mixed results, and red for well behind plan. During the quarterly 1:1, the manager and employee reach mutual agreement on each the employee's assessments of progress by addressing the 4 After-Action Review questions. The discussion then shifts to the proposed tasks on the Implementation Plan for the next quarter. Like strategic planning, each quarter should move the employee closer to the Definitions of Success they established at the beginning of the year.

After-Action Review Questions

What was supposed to happen?

What actually happened?

Why was there a difference?

What can you learn from this?

Desired Outcome

We adopted a definition of **performance management** as an ongoing process of communication between a supervisor and an employee that occurs routinely throughout the year, in support of accomplishing mutually accepted and quantifiable personal goals that are in alignment with the strategic objectives of the company. The process to accomplish this involves reaching Clarity and Focus on the Top 6 Roles and associated critical results. This input is used in an Implementation Plan that establishes a specific, measurable, and achievable Plan of Action for each quarter, so that small steps move towards longer-term goals and success can be celebrated along the way. Effectively conducted regular 1:1s keep communication high and encourage mutual commitment towards success. In the end, effective communication is at the core of performance management. For additional insights, readers are encouraged to download the Vistage Research report Performance Management: Communicating Expectations and Evaluations.[23]

Summary

Efficient and effective *executing on culture* requires vigilance and discipline. The key to *Executing on Culture* is to focus specifically on two things: 1) the role culture plays in recruiting and 2) developing talent in a positive culture of accountability.

In our discussion of executing on culture we have focused on getting the right people onto the bus during the recruiting phase through use of cultural assessments and cultural interviewing. We also focused on keeping people individually engaged and working together with their peers in pursuit of the common good of the organization through an integrated performance management system. Combined, these human systems encourage ordinary people to achieve extraordinary results.

Recall the neuropsychology of human behavior introduced in chapter 4 that suggests that our emotions and feelings influence our beliefs, that those beliefs drive our actions and behaviors, and in turn ultimately produce results and outcomes. Dale Carnegie outlined nine principles for how to change people without giving offense or arousing resentment, one of which was "Give the other person a fine reputation to live up to."[24] Tell your people what you are trying to achieve, explain the importance of their contributions to these goals, train and skill them to be effective, and then invest confidence. The systems described in this chapter on *executing on culture* are built upon the neuropsychology of human behavior and help realize this timeless principle of Dale Carnegie.

Chapter 14

EXECUTING ON STRATEGY

We defined Strategy as the art and science of deploying resources to achieve stated goals or objectives of the organization at an enterprise, business unit, or product or service line level. Strategy describes in broad terms how goals are to be achieved and marshals the resources (people, time, money) for their most efficient and effective use. Strategy requires a well-developed roadmap for getting to the desired destination, and in Recipe for Business Success, this roadmap is the outcome of a rigorous strategic planning process.

We defined strategic planning as an ongoing process that creates the roadmap, or Strategy, for moving from a well-defined Present State to a compelling and different Future State. In chapter 9 we provided an overview of the process used to define the Present State, envision and describe the desired Future State, and develop and implement the Strategy for getting there (i.e., the Plan for Success). The remaining action for fully *Executing on Strategy* is to review the strategic planning cycle necessary to ensure it remains an ongoing process, keeps things moving forward, and promotes accountability while allowing for course corrections as circumstances change.

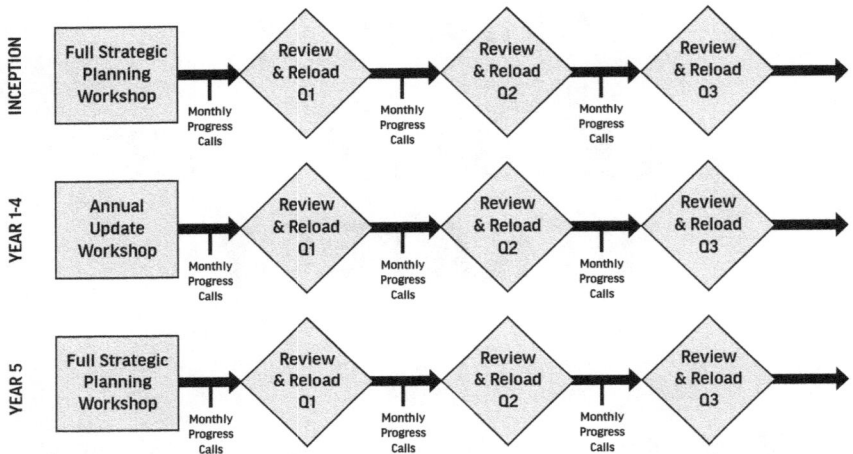

Figure 14.1: Strategic planning implementation timeline

Some explanation of the three main (and recurring) elements illustrated in Fig. 14.1 is warranted. That is, the full strategic planning (SP) workshop, the quarterly Review & Reloads sessions, and the annual SP update.

Full Strategic Planning Workshop

In our suggested model, the Full Strategic Planning (SP) Workshop occurs once every 3-5 years. As suggested in chapter 9, the Full SP Workshop may be completed over a series of consecutive days (likely 2-plus days), but the preferred method is to utilize 3 shorter meetings on separate days, each focused on:

1. Review of all Present State information and SWOT Analysis
2. Development of the Vision statement and long-term (3-5 year) Overarching goals
3. Development of 1-year Key Strategic Initiatives and Definitions of Success

During the first session of a 3-session format, the participants confirm and recommit to the Core Ideology. The balance and majority of the time is spent developing a common understanding of all aspects of the present state of organizational health and business environment before completing the SWOT analysis to gain agreement on current Strengths, Weaknesses, Opportunities and Threats. During the second session and with the outcomes of the SWOT Analysis in mind, participants create the timeless Vision statement (or challenge an existing one to make certain it remains relevant), create the optional North Star statement, and establish specific Overarching Goals for the next 3-5 years. That is, participants paint a verbal picture of the desired destination. The third session deals with development of the Plan for Success, including gaining group consensus on draft Key Strategic Initiatives for the upcoming year and selecting a Champion to chair the initiative. As described in chapter 9, the Champion will recruit members of their team. This Key Strategy (KS) team will finalize the objective and Definitions of Success for their key strategy, and ultimately reflect the tasks for the first 90 days on the Implementation Plan used to guide all strategic planning participants along the journey.

The duration of full strategic planning workshops at the business unit or product or service line level will vary, depending upon the complexity of the operations, magnitude of current undertakings, and availability of key stakeholders needed for an effective planning session. However, in nearly all circumstances, a full strategic planning workshop will require at least a full day – or 3 shorter meetings similar to those described above. While the durations may vary, the scope of topics undertaken, and the general process followed, are similar to that described above for the entire enterprise.

Review & Reload

As illustrated in Fig. 14.1, Review & Reload (R&R) sessions should be scheduled at approximately, 90, 180, and 270 days after conclusion of the SP workshop. Strategies fail if allowed to become static or not subjected to review. A formal R&R process is necessary to keep the organization heading in the right direction, while allowing course corrections to address current circumstances. The R&R process ensures that strategy is dynamic. At a minimum, monthly calls among each Key Strategy (KS) team are deemed essential. The monthly calls keep team members focused on the tasks outlined on the Implementation Plan.

The actual R&R session normally requires about 30 minutes per Key Strategy. All participants from the SP workshop, and any new participants added to the KS teams, should be present. A rectangular set up of tables allows for 'face-to-face' conversations. Open conversations among participants are encouraged. Use of formal presentations is discouraged. Each participant should have a copy of the strategic plan (see template in Appendix 2.2), the current Implementation Plan, and the proposed Implementation Plan for the next 90 days. As previously described, the KS Champion should address the four After-Action Review questions:

What was supposed to happen?
What actually happened?
Why was there a difference?
What can we learn from this?

The tasks for a given KS as outlined in the current Implementation Plan help describe "What was supposed to happen." And the color coding each task for a given KS as white (Complete), Green (In-progress and on track), Yellow (some wheelspin), and Red (little to no progress) help describe "What actually happened." The real conversation should revolve around exploring "Why was there a difference." In a positive culture of accountability, this does not involve below-the-line excuses or rationalizations. Instead, it is a frank conversation involving recognizing reality (i.e., See It), accepting shared responsibility across the team (i.e., Own It), outlining a plan forward from "What we learned" (i.e., Solve It). This is followed by a discussion of the tasks (actions and risk) in the Implementation Plan for the next 90 days (i.e., Do It).

As can be recognized, the R&R process is intentionally designed to monitor progress, make necessary course corrections, and most importantly, reinforce the desired positive culture of accountability. The experience of the participants during the R&R session will influence their beliefs about leadership's commitment to openness, mutual respect, and accountability, which in turn will influence their behaviors, and ultimately lead to the desired results. The facilitator of the R&R session must adapt a leadership style appropriate to these circumstances.

Annual Update Workshop

The cycle outlined in Fig. 14.1 reflects an Annual SP Update workshop. Annual SP Update workshops should be scheduled as close as reasonable to the anniversary of the Full Strategic Planning Workshop. There will be two annual update workshops with a 3-year overall planning cycle, and four annual update workshops with a 5-year overall planning cycle. Each annual update workshop should follow an agenda similar to the full workshop, but with a differing level of depth.

The Present State information (i.e., Current Initiatives, Survey Input, and Analytics) from the previous year should be updated and discussed. New information can be added if/as warranted. The "Current Initiatives" portion of the discussion should include a final R&R session on the current year's Key Strategies (KS). There are two important changes to the final year-end R&R process. First, the litmus test against which progress is measured (i.e., What was supposed to happen?) are the Definitions of Success for each KS that were established one year earlier (i.e., **not** the tasks on the final Implementation Plan). Second, while the four After-Action Review questions remain the same, a fifth question is added – What remains to be done to bring this KS, as defined, to conclusion? That is, if any of the Definitions of Success that were established for a KS during the previous year's workshop remain open, the work necessary to close it out should be explored. This does not mean that the KS will carry over for another year. It simply allows consideration of bringing any open KS to reasonable conclusion before determining what the Key Strategies will be in the upcoming year.

The Vision, North Star, and Overarching Goals are challenged during an Annual SP Update workshop, but not changed unless something within the realm of organizational health or business environment has changed to such a significant degree to warrant reconsideration of previously vetted descriptors of the desired Future State.

The main focus during the Annual SP Update workshop is on the Plan for Success (Strategy) for the next year. The process to arrive at the Key Strategies and Definitions of Success for the next year was fully described in chapter 9 and is identical to that outlined for the Full SP Workshop above. However, when arriving at the new Key Strategies, consideration must be given to the extent of progress made towards accomplishing the long-term (3-5 year) Overarching Goals. As outlined in chapter 9, the new Plan for Success should move the organization 1 year closer to those long-term goals. Line of sight to the desired destination must be maintained or effort may be unnecessarily expended on a current initiative that does not materially contribute to closing the gap 'from where we are now to where we want to be.'

Line of sight to the desired destination must be maintained or effort may be unnecessarily expended on a current initiative that does not materially contribute to closing the gap 'from where we are now to where we want to be.'

The dates for another cycle of R&R meetings should be agreed upon at the conclusion of the Annual SP Update workshop. Establishing a formal calendar further reinforces the positive culture of accountability that is the underlying prerequisite to success with *Executing on Strategy*.

Summary

Strategic planning is an ongoing process – not an event. And the resultant Plan for Success (Strategy) must be continuously challenged. During the strategic planning process, participants listen to, analyze, and debate data and information until reaching a common understanding of the Present State of organizational health and the business environment. With this knowledge in hand, verbal pictures of a compelling Future State and the roadmap for getting there are created. But like having a riderless bicycle, the Strategy will be of little use without aggressive Execution by an engaged workforce that embraces a positive culture of accountability.

Successful execution of the Strategy is critical. The Strategic Planning implementation timeline in general, and the annual Plan for Success process specifically, create the roadmap to move towards defined Overarching Goals. The Strategy includes key strategic initiatives for the next year, an Implementation Plan tool to identity and focus on the most important short-term tasks, and a robust Review & Reload process that helps establish accountability, monitor progress, and make course corrections as necessary. Every element of the timeline illustrated in Fig. 14.1 must be addressed to efficiently and effectively *Execute on Strategy*.

There are three different roles for all those involved in the ongoing implementation of the strategic planning process.

- The facilitator selected to bring about desired outcomes plans, guides, and manages the group. The facilitator '***owns the process***.'
- Participants actively engage in each/all the major elements described above, including ongoing contributions to key strategic initiatives each year. Participants '***own the plan***' (i.e., the resulting strategy).

- The senior executive involved (e.g., CEO or Executive Director) 'calls the shot' when full consensus is in question, approves the plan (or seeks approval from a board of directors), coach's participants, and commits resources (people, time, money) as necessary to ensure success. The senior executive is the ultimate servant leader and '*owns accountability*' for outcomes.

Put succinctly, the facilitator manages the process, participants own and implement the resultant plan, while the senior executive removes barriers to success and keeps the group's behaviors 'above the line' (i.e., See It, Own It, Solve It, Do It) to ensure success.

Chapter 15

TOP TAKEAWAYS AND TIPS

CASE STUDY – THE ASCEND SUMMIT LLC STORY

On the first day of ASCEND's 2018 strategic planning workshop, the team defined their Core Ideology by creating Core Purpose, Core Values, and Mission Statements (see chapter 5 for a summary of that process) during the morning session. They then drafted an initial Vision Statement and established Overarching Goals during the afternoon session.

On the morning of day two of the workshop, which occurred five weeks later, the initial Core Ideology and Overarching Goals were challenged and finalized. The balance of day two was spent developing the Plan for Success for the upcoming year (see chapter 10 for a summary of that process). The discussion that follows describes how the leadership of ASCEND executed their plan and maintained an ongoing strategic planning process.

Annual SP Update Workshops

ASCEND adopted the overall SP implementation timeline outlined in Fig. 14.1 of Chapter 14: *Executing* on Strategy. The very first Full SP Workshop was completed in May 2018, and the plan was reviewed and approved by the Board of Managers just weeks later. While the board offered constructive insights, no substantive changes were made. The initial Strategic Plan was officially adopted in June. Quarterly R&R sessions were scheduled at 90, 180, and 270 days following approval of the Plan. The timeframe for the first annual SP Update Workshop was shifted by two months to better align with budgeting and program planning for the subsequent year. Annual update workshops were conducted during July of 2019, 2020, and 2021. Each of the annual update workshops followed an agenda similar to the topical headings addressed during the initial full meeting, with some notable differences:

- The range of participants expanded with each annual update to the point where a full range of "Influencers" were engaged in the process by 2021. The management team had shifted from a top-down to a cross-organizational scheme of planning (as described in Chapter 7: Strategic Planning Processes) which was more in line with the intentionally emerging participatory and authentic culture (as described in Chapter 4: Achieving Desired Culture).

- Each annual update started with a review and reconfirmation of the ASCEND Core Ideology. Because of the expanding range of participants, cognitive diversity increased, and new perspectives drove some minor changes. The same can be said of the Vision and Overarching Goals, where input from an increasingly diverse group led to some edits and clarifications. The resulting Strategic Plan that evolved is included as Appendix 1.

- The breadth and depth of information processed during the Present State discussions increased and improved. Certain previously confidential financial metrics were shared. Final After-Action Reports on the previous year's key strategies were debated. Outcomes from formal surveys of members and staff were reviewed. With this as background, the original lists of Top 5 Strengths, Weaknesses, Opportunities, and Threats were updated each year to reflect current realities. An evolving "track change" version of the SWOT Analysis was appended to the Plan each year.

- Following the review and confirmation of the existing Vision and Overarching Goals, the expanded team of participants created the enterprise-wide key strategies for the upcoming year.

Beyond the above, the most dramatic difference within the first 4-year planning cycle was undoubtedly the onset and lengthy recovery from Covid-19. The adverse impacts on indoor fitness businesses cannot be overstated. ASCEND management used the ongoing nature of effective strategic planning to make necessary course corrections. These corrections mainly impacted the nature of annual key strategic initiatives during 2020 and 2021. To management's credit, no change was made to the Overarching Goals that remained as the verbal picture of ASCEND for June 2022. Despite Covid, after a full analysis of the Present State, the broad group of participants in the second Full SP Workshop conducted in July 2022 awarded a B⁺ grade for progress made on achieving the Overarching Goals set 4-years earlier by the founders.

Second Full SP Workshop

The second full SP workshop was conducted in June/July 2022. There were three interrelated changes made before the workshop was conducted.

1. The range of participants selected for the workshop included key managers, supervisors, and influencers for each area of programming (e.g., route setting, yoga, youth, etc.), each existing and pending location (e.g., ASCEND Pittsburgh, ASCEND Youngstown, etc.) and each area of operations (e.g., finance, human resources, marketing, etc.).

2. To create the uninterrupted time required for strategic planning, the workshop was conducted over 3 shorter sessions separated by 2-week intervals, focusing on:
   a. Review of all Present State information and SWOT Analysis
   b. Challenging the Vision statement and developing long-term (4-year) Overarching Goals
   c. Development of 1-year Key Strategic Initiatives and Definitions of Success

3. To accommodate the more protracted scheduling and as part of the ongoing development of his leadership practice, Alex Bernstein, Founder and Director of Finance and Business Development, assumed the role of facilitator.

Naturally, the content of the current strategic plan is confidential and will not be discussed. It can be said that in the eyes of the Board of

Managers, the outcome of the effort was quite successful. ASCEND has a new, exceptional business strategy built upon the organization's culture, and the organizational culture is aligned with and supportive of the business strategy. In the language of Recipe for Business Success, ASCEND is poised for ongoing "Success," of conducting a lawful, ethical, profitable, and sustainable business that grows value for all stakeholders over the long term while embracing environmental, social, and governance (ESG) responsibilities. An annotated template for a similarly structured strategic plan is included as Appendix 2.2.

Top 10 Takeaways for Part III

1. There are prerequisites for a chef working to prepare a fabulous meal. Likewise, there are three prerequisites necessary to prepare for the Execution ingredient in our Recipe for Business Success.

2. As a first prerequisite, efficient and effective Execution of both culture and strategic plans requires establishing a positive culture of accountability by changing paradigms about owning outcomes (the Oz Principle), and creating clarity and focus on desired organizational and individual outcomes (Plan for Success).

3. A servant leader is someone who identifies and meets the legitimate needs of their people, removes all the barriers to their success, so they can serve their customers. The role of an intentional servant leader is to help ordinary people achieve extraordinary results. Adopting an intentional servant leadership style easily facilitates fulfillment of the second prerequisite of aligning leadership practices with the intended Culture and Strategy.

4. The third prerequisite to sustaining efficient and effective Execution requires leadership to embrace lifelong learning to remain agile and open-minded during an era of exponential rate of change through intentionally developing their leadership practice.

5. A key to executing on culture is to focus specifically on the role culture plays in recruiting and developing talent in a positive culture of accountability.

6. There are three components of every person that factor into their likely success at a given job. These include cognitive capability (IQ), emotional intelligence (EQ), and the personality type/style that defines each of us.

7. Candidates must possess desired core competencies to get a seat on the bus. But the more difficult and more important question is, Can the core competencies be brought to bear in the specific situational fit of the organization's work environment and culture?

8. Performance management is an ongoing process of communication between a supervisor and an employee that occurs routinely throughout the year, in support of accomplishing mutually accepted and quantifiable personal goals that are in alignment with the strategic objectives of the company.

9. Fully executing on strategy requires adoption of an overall strategic planning cycle to ensure the planning remains an ongoing process, keeps things moving forward, and promotes accountability while allowing for course corrections as circumstances change.

10. The facilitator owns the process, the participants own the plan, and the chief executive owns accountability for outcomes.

Top 10 Tips for Implementing Part III

1. Efficient execution requires working in a well-organized and competent way to achieve maximum productivity with minimum wasted effort or expense. Effective execution requires focus on specifically desired goals and intended results. Both require vigilance and discipline, and both are needed to achieve success.

2. Consider your inventory of available leadership skills as a toolbox. Commit to lifelong learning to expand the depth and breadth of your skills as part of an intentional leadership practice. Do the same with those you lead. Reading, and specifically interactive book clubs and formal debates, help expand horizons.

3. Survey tools for assessing IQ, EQ and/or personality type may play a role in assessing the situational fit of a candidate with respect to the work environment and culture, but they are best used to inform the questions to be explored during the actual interviewing process rather than stringent Go/No Go criteria.

4. Getting the right people on the bus is the first step; promotion of a positive culture of accountability and adoption of desired cultural norms is the second, never-ending step. A comprehensive performance management system helps guarantee the clarity and focus required for personal accountability and ensuring desired behaviors throughout an employee's career.

5. There is a degree of efficiency achieved when similar business processes can be adapted for multiple beneficial uses. The Plan for Success model of establishing objectives, definitions of success, and formalized review and reload, is appliable to

organizational strategies, project management, and individual performance management.

6. The essential ingredient for a performance management system to work is to have goals which are not only mutually agreed upon and well defined but are also quantifiable.

7. The linchpin of the ongoing process of communication between a supervisor and an employee is the formalized monthly 1:1 meetings and quarterly review & reload sessions. If 'employees are your greatest asset,' invest your time in them.

8. Each annual strategic plan update workshop should follow an agenda similar to the full workshop, but with a differing level of depth for all elements except the annual Plan for Success.

9. The preferred method to utilize for strategic planning is 3 shorter meetings on separate days, each focused on:

    a. Review of all Present State information and SWOT Analysis

    b. Development of the Vision statement and long-term (3-5-year) Overarching goals

    c. Development of 1-year Key Strategic Initiatives and Definitions of Success

10. Allow the Recipe for Business Success to challenge your existing paradigms, focus your attention on three essential ingredients to success, identify actionable takeaways, and contribute to your individual and organizational success.

Citations and References

PART III – Execution

1. For more information on famous and inspirational quotes see BrainyQuote, https://www.brainyquote.com/; Quote Investigator, https://quoteinvestigator.com/.

2. See Merriam-Webster, https://www.merriam-webster.com/.

3. Deborah Easton, "Are You Defining 'Accountability' Correctly?," Center for Corporate and Professional Development, Kent State University, January 18 2017, https://www.kent.edu/yourtrainingpartner/are-you-defining-accountability-correctly.

4. Roger Connors, Tom Smith, and Craig Hickman, *The Oz Principle: Getting Results Through Individual and Organizational Accountability* (New York: Portfolio, 2004).

5. For more information on leadership style assessments see Kodzo Agbesi, "Top 10 Leadership Assessment Tools for 2022," *Journey to Leadership* (blog), September 30, 2021, *https://journeytoleadershipblog.com/2021/09/30/top-10-leadership-assessment-tool/*.

6. Robert Greenleaf, "The Servant as Leader," *Servant Leadership: A Journey into the Nature and Legitimate Power of Greatness* (New York: Paulist Press, 1977), http://www.ediguys.net/Robert_K_Greenleaf_The_Servant_as_Leader.pdf.

7. Leo Tilman and Charles Jacoby, *Agility: How to Navigate the Unknown and Seize Opportunity in a World of Disruption* (Arlington, VA: Missionday, 2019).

8. Shane Snow, *Dream Teams: Working Together without Falling Apart* (New York: Portfolio/Penguin, 2018).

9. See guidelines for "Conducting a Debate," Manitoba (website), accessed February 5, 2023, https://www.edu.gov.mb.ca/k12/cur/socstud/frame_found_sr2/tns/tn-13.pdf.

10. Peter W. Schutz, *The Driving Force: Extraordinary Results with Ordinary People* (Naples, FL: LeadershipPublishing.com/Harris & Schutz, 2005).

11. Jim Collins, *Good to Great: Why Some Companies Make the Leap...and Others Don't* (New York: HarperBusiness, 2001).

12. Travis Bradberry and Jean Greaves, *Emotional Intelligence 2.0* (San Diego: TalentSmart, 2009).

13. See "MBTI® Basics," My MBTI ® Personality Type, The Myers & Briggs Foundation, accessed February 5, 2023, https://www.myersbriggs.org/my-mbti-personality-type/mbti-basics/.

14. Kendra Cherry, "How the Myers-Briggs Type Indicator Works," Verywell Mind, updated July 28, 2022, https://www.verywellmind.com/the-myers-briggs-type-indicator-2795583.

15. Nicole Fallon, "What Kind of Leader Are You?," Business News Daily, updated January 23, 2023, https://www.businessnewsdaily.com/8692-disc-assessment.html.

16. Janet Boydell, Barry Deutsch, and Brad Remillard, *You're NOT the Person I Hired!: A CEO's Survival Guide to Hiring Top Talent* (Bloomington, IN: AuthorHouse, 2006).

17. Lou Adler, *The Essential Guide for Hiring & Getting Hired* (self-pub., 2013).

18. See the article "What You Need to Know About Performance Appraisals," Society for Human Resource Management, https://www.shrm.org/resourcesandtools/tools-and-samples/need-to-know/pages/what-you-need-to-know-about-performance-appraisals.aspx.

19. Adam Hayes, "Performance Appraisals in the Workplace: Use, Types, Criticisms," Investopedia, updated October 23, 2022, https://www.investopedia.com/what-is-a-performance-appraisal-4586834.

20. See "Performance Management: Concepts & Definitions," People and Culture, University of California, Berkeley, accessed February 5, 2023, https://hr.berkeley.edu/hr-network/central-guide-managing-hr/managing-hr/managing-successfully/performance-management/concepts.

21. Julia Smith, FCIPD, MBPsS, "Clarity...The Unsung Hero of New Performance Management," LinkedIn, January 16, 2019, https://www.linkedin.com/pulse/claritythe-unsung-hero-new-performance-management-julia-smith/.

22. David Bishton, "5 Benefits of How a Focus on Ensuring Clarity Drives Improvement," LinkedIn, October 2, 2020, https://www.linkedin.com/pulse/5-benefits-how-focus-ensuring-clarity-drives-dave-bishton/.

23. See Vistage's Research & Insights "Explore by Category," Research and Insights, Vistage Worldwide, Inc., accessed February 5, 2023, https://www.vistage.com/research-center/business-leadership/; specifically Joe Galvin, "Performance Management: Communicating Expectations and Evaluations," Research and Insights, Vistage Worldwide, Inc., March 14, 2017, https://www.vistage.com/research-center/talent-management/human-resources/20170316-performance-management-communicating-expectations-evaluations/.

24. Dale Carnegie, *How to Win Friends and Influence People – Revised Edition*, ed. Dorothy Carnegie and Arthur R. Pell (New York: Simon and Schuster, 1981).

Additional Resources

In addition to the specific sources outlined above, internet searches on the following topical headings will provide a wealth of additional information and insights on the topics discussed in Part III:

- Accountability in the workplace
- Leadership styles
- Servant Leadership
- Intentional Leadership
- Culture interview questions
- Personality Assessments in the workplace
- Performance Management
- Executing on strategy
- Coaching Skills for Leaders

EPILOGUE

If we think about Culture, Strategy, and Execution as essential ingredients in a Recipe for Business Success, it is important to note that the "mix" of ingredients is not fixed. In our recipe for success, the chef (aka CEO or Executive Director) must determine the right mix of these essential ingredients and select the special seasonings to make the perfect meal. The emphasis may shift from strategy, to execution, to culture, dependent upon where the organization (enterprise, business unit, or product or service) is on its lifecycle, and what is needed to achieve "Success." That is, to conduct a lawful, ethical, profitable, and sustainable business to grow value for stakeholders over the long term while embracing social, environmental, and governance responsibilities.

BUSINESS PRODUCT/SERVICE LIFE CYCLE

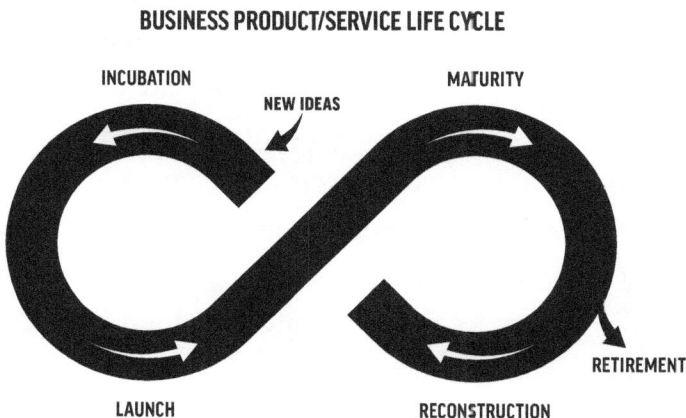

INCUBATION   NEW IDEAS   MATURITY

LAUNCH   RECONSTRUCTION   RETIREMENT

Put differently, there will be points in the illustrated business or product lifecycle when the greatest focus may be on developing strategy (e.g., prior to initial launch) or maintaining an intentional culture (e.g., throughout the entire maturity phase), or aggressive execution (e.g., following reconstruction of an enterprise, business unit, or product or service line). Leadership must continually survey organizational health and business environment while exercising agility in shifting emphasis among the essential ingredients.

Culture

SUCCESS

Strategy   Execution

Just as winemaking never follows some strict recipe, there is no perfect blend of ingredients in our Recipe for Business Success. And while the winemaker might source the best cabernet sauvignon, merlot, and cabernet franc grapes as the essential varietals for their red blend, it is the smaller portions of malbec, petit verdot, and carménère that result in the finest meritage. The special seasonings in our Recipe for Business Success include having a positive culture of accountability, alignment of leadership practices to strategy and culture, and commitment to lifelong learning. The intentional servant leader that is committed to our definition of success embraces these seasonings and pursues other special herbs and spices as part of developing their leadership practice to complement the main ingredients and continually recreate their perfect dish. At a minimum:

For the *Culture* ingredient, the Recipe for Business Success calls for:

- Fully embracing the fact that people are every organization's greatest asset. There are no exceptions. You can have protected intellectual property, unique processes, or phenomenal brands, but without people, there is nothing.
- Recognizing that every time there is an introduction of a new generation into the workforce, or simply new hiring, transfers, promotions, or changes in processes, there is the opportunity for new cultural norms to emerge.
- Creating experiences to solicit the specific emotions and feelings supportive of desired beliefs, which drive desired behaviors, and result in desired outcomes.
- Starting by intentionally designing a core ideology, aligning actions and experiences with words, and continual re-creation in an unending dynamic cycle.

For the *Strategy* ingredient, the Recipe for Business Success calls for:

- Evaluating the numerous models available for strategic planning.
- Selecting one that:
    - is an ongoing process,
    - creates a roadmap (strategy),
    - for getting the organization from a well-defined Present State,
    - to a compelling and different Future state.

- Adopting and embracing the tools and process to support ongoing execution of the Strategy.

For the *Execution* ingredient, the Recipe for Business Success calls for:

- Firmly establishing the mix of prerequisites required for efficient and effective execution including:
  - a positive culture of accountability,
  - aligning leadership practices with the intended Culture and Strategy, and
  - embracing lifelong learning to remain agile and open-minded.
- Recognizing that strategic planning is an ongoing process – not an event; the resultant Plan for Success (Strategy) must be continuously challenged.
- Focusing specifically on the role culture plays in recruiting and developing talent in a positive culture of accountability, and
- Keeping people engaged and working together with their peers in pursuit of the common good of the organization through a fully integrated performance management system.

Recall from the illustration in the Introduction to Part I, that Strategy is depicted as the front wheel, fork and handlebars of a bike. It is used to set direction for where the organization is headed and make necessary course corrections. Culture is depicted as the chain, cogs, and back wheel. Culture provides the drive train to move the organization forward. But without a rider, the bike doesn't move. Alternatively, without Execution, the best laid plan will never be implemented and the benefits of an aligned culture will never be realized.

In their Spring 2022 magazine Trek Bicycle suggested in an article *The Fast Factory*, that at the legendary Trek Race Shop in Waterloo, WI, only greatness is accepted. "It's athletes who win races. But they often don't win on equipment that hasn't been meticulously tuned to their exacting preferences."

Business strategy must be built upon an organization's culture, and the organization's culture must be aligned with and supportive of the business strategy. And as Trek suggests, both must be tuned with exacting precision to get extraordinary results from ordinary people.

In conclusion, Culture, Strategy, and Execution are parts of an integrated system. Business success is far more likely to occur when a relevant plan (Strategy) is aggressively implemented (Execution) by a fully engaged workforce (Culture). They must work together in unison to achieve the desired Success of *conducting a lawful, ethical, profitable, and sustainable business to grow value for stakeholders over the long term while embracing social, environmental, and governance responsibility.*

ACKNOWLEDGMENTS

I t wasn't until sometime in middle age, that period between adulthood and approaching retirement, that I recognized a trait that I had carried with me throughout my career: I enjoyed and was committed to lifelong learning. And I feel compelled to acknowledge and give credit to those that instilled this wonderful value.

I attended St. Vincent College, a liberal arts school in Latrobe, Pennsylvania, but certainly never appreciated just how much those studies of the humanities and social sciences would complement my degree in chemistry and serve me throughout my career. I am eternally grateful to the Benedictines, faculty, and administration for the value and strong emphasis they placed on experiencing a liberal arts education.

My first job out of college was with the Loss Prevention Department of Liberty Mutual Insurance Company, the largest writer of workers' compensation insurance and one of the nation's largest property and casualty insurance carriers at the time. In the first eighteen months of employment, I had completed both Basic and Intermediate (Phase I and II) Training, and in the next eighteen months I availed myself of nearly every Phase III - Advanced training program even in specialties outside of my immediate area of interest. I also availed myself of training in related insurance disciplines like underwriting and sales. Much of this training was part of the ordinary plan for any loss prevention representative, but at management's encouragement, I also pursued many extra programs. It wasn't like I did this with any clear intent. That is, the training wasn't to qualify me for the next promotion. Without really recognizing it, I was learning for the sake of learning, and I have Liberty Mutual to thank.

While assuming various leadership roles at KTA, I benefited immensely from participating over a fifteen-plus year period in the key executive and CEO programs of Vistage. The shared expertise and critical issue processing with my peers, tremendous monthly coaching with Arvind Paranjpe, our group chair, and presentations from over 120 renowned experts in vastly verifying fields all pushed the boundaries of my perspective and contributed incalculably to my development as a leader.

Commitment to the continual pursuit of lifelong learning has served me well in my forty-five years in business. Working with and being mentored by many wonderful professionals in both the for-profit and not-for-profit arenas has been invaluable. It awakened a need to be open-minded—willing to change opinions in the face of compelling evidence to the contrary and being critically receptive to alternative possibilities. It caused me to filter through the static and remain focused on what is truly most important. The specific names and contributions of all those that helped shape my experience are far too many to list. However, I am especially grateful to the key mentors and supporters that I drew upon to read my earliest manuscript. They deserve recognition for their great insights and contributions to this work.

Robert H. Chalker - CEO of The Association for Materials Protection and Performance (AMP) following the merger of

NACE International and the Society for Protective Coatings (SSPC), and active board member of nonprofit associations

E. Joeseph Duckett, Ph.D., P.E. – author, former executive, active board member of for-profit and nonprofit organizations, and appointed member of numerous government environmental advisory committees

David W. McFayden – CEO of KTA-Tator, Inc., the 100-percent employee-owned nationwide materials engineering firm upon which much of this work was modeled

Kenneth A. Trimber – author, and former President and current Chairman of KTA-Tator Inc. board of directors

Amy Veltri, P.E. – Co-Founder and CEO at NGE Consulting, an employee-owned highly specialized environmental and geotechnical small business

This book would not have been published in its final form without the insights and editorial support of Eland R. Mann, co-founder of Conversation Publishing, and graphics and design work of George B. Stevens, founder and designer at G Sharp Design. I also owe a debt of gratitude to Alex Bernstein, Paul Guarino, Aaron Gilmore for allowing me to share the story of ASCEND Summit LLC and how they used concepts described in Recipe for Business Success as an integrated part of their business processes.

I have been blessed with a meaningful, fulfilling, and rewarding life and career. I hope I might *help improve the lives of others* (my personal

"Why") by writing this book. I do not seek personal gain. My intent is to donate proceeds from this book to our family's charitable trust.

APPENDIX 1

Example Plan: ASCEND Summit LLC.

The following is the actual strategic plan that resulted from the planning process summarized in the ASCEND Story in chapters 5, 10, and 15.

ASCEND STRATEGIC PLAN FOR 2022

At ASCEND, strategic planning is an ongoing process designed to provide a roadmap for taking us from a well-defined Present State to a compelling and significantly different Future State. The narrative on the pages that follow describes our roadmap for taking us from where we are in May 2018 to just after our 5-year anniversary in July 2022.

All our strategic initiatives are framed by our Core Ideology. Our Core Ideology defines who we are. It includes a statement of Core Purpose, which establishes *why we exist* in the marketplace; our noble cause. It includes our Core Values, which establish *how we behave*. And it includes our Mission, which outlines *what it is we do*. Taken collectively, our Core Purpose, Core Values, and Mission reflect the ideology that makes *ASCEND* a premiere climbing and fitness community.

Our Core Purpose

To provide a healthy, lifestyle-based, alternative fitness experience in an accessible, climbing-focused, and community-centered environment.

Our Core Values

Accessible — We strive to ensure equitable access to climbing and approachability of our organization, whether it be in our facilities or the outdoors.

Authentic — We put ourselves, honestly and uniquely, into our work.

Passionate — We are actively engaged in the climbing lifestyle, acting as stewards of the spaces we occupy, especially through environmental awareness and community collaboration.

Hardworking — We value strong work ethics, while recognizing that people have different strengths.

Our Mission

ASCEND fosters an equitable, holistic, community-based, climbing, fitness, and yoga experience.

The first step of creating a roadmap to a compelling and significantly different Future State is to define our Vision of the future. Vision describes *what we want to become.* It is a timeless statement that is both aspirational, and inspirational for our owners and associates.

Our Vision

ASCEND is nationally recognized as an industry influencer, integrating leading edge technology, equipment, and programming to provide equitable access to all climbing disciplines, while serving as the most inclusive employer and fitness community in the markets we serve.

The overarching goals set in May 2018 created a verbal picture of what ASCEND will look like in June 2022. Achieving these goals moves us toward and embodies the spirit of our Vision.

Our Overarching Goals for June 2022

Growth/Expansion
- ASCEND has three or four full-service facilities in Southwestern PA operating with acceptable financial performance and uses an evaluation model to assess growth options in real time.

Operational Excellence
- ASCEND has achieved operational excellence by way of consistently implemented systems and processes reflected in well-defined job functions throughout the company.

Comprehensive Youth Program

- ASCEND has spearheaded and helps foster a robust, inclusive, full-scope regional youth climbing competition experience, including a competitive team with dedicated training facilities.

Expanded Outdoor Program

- ASCEND operates a seasonal outdoor guiding program, leading regional day trips, weekend excursions, and all-inclusive retreats.

Philanthropy, Equity, and Access

- ASCEND responsibly deploys financial, human, and other available resources through structured channels to a wide-array of individuals, organizations, and causes, with a focus on facilitating equitable access.

ASCEND PITTSBURGH
PLAN FOR SUCCESS
Our Key Strategies for 2021-2022

Based upon the foundation of our Core Ideology, the Board of Managers of ASCEND Pittsburgh approved three (3) Key Strategies developed by the leadership team for the period of July 1, 2021 to June 30, 2022. These Key Strategic initiatives are designed to fulfill our Vision and realize our Overarching Goals for July 2022.

The specific Key Strategies and Definitions of Success for the current planning year follow. A separate one-page Traction Plan is maintained, defining the specific steps to be taken to achieve the Definitions of Success for each Key Strategy in the next year, broken down into 90-day increments.

[The actual Key Strategies contain confidential information and are not reproduced.]

APPENDIX 2.1

Strategic Envisioning Workshop:
Data Collection Form

What are the top 20 questions that need to be addressed to provide direction and create a compelling vision of the future for our organization?

1. _____
2. _____
3. _____
4. _____
5. _____
6. _____
7. _____
8. _____
9. _____
10. _____
11. _____
12. _____
13. _____
14. _____
15. _____
16. _____
17. _____
18. _____
19. _____
20. _____

If everything is important, then nothing is. In your mind, what are the top 3 questions from the above list?

1. _____
2. _____
3. _____

Identify each/every participant's "top 3" questions on the list of 20 questions above. Which questions were selected the most times? As a group, determine the top 5 questions the group needs to explore further?

1. _____
2. _____
3. _____
4. _____
5. _____

After studying the Top 5 questions outlined above, look for questions that suggest new pathways. Create (one or two) questions that fully 'reframe' the problem and provide new angles for solving it.

1. _____
2. _____

Expand/unpack reframed question #1 using the "5 whys."

1. _____
2. _____
3. _____
4. _____
5. _____

Expand/unpack reframed question #2 using the "5 whys."

1. _____
2. _____
3. _____
4. _____
5. _____

Catalytic Questions

Study the reframed questions and the responses to the 5-Whys. What catalytic questions do we really need to answer? That is, questions that dissolve barriers to creative thinking and channel pursuit of solutions into new pathways? The questions that dramatically change the range of possible solutions are:

1. _____
2. _____

Inside of every question is a 'quest.' Strategic planning participants will need to define the quest – the pursuit of one or two new pathways – to answer these catalytic questions.

APPENDIX 2.2

TEMPLATE STRATEGIC PLAN

~ORGANIZATION'S NAME~
STRATEGIC PLAN – 20YY

Strategic planning is an ongoing process designed to provide a roadmap for taking us from a well-defined Present State to a compelling and significantly different Future State. The narrative on the pages that follow describes our goals for 20YY and our plan for getting there. All our strategic initiatives are framed by our Core Ideology. Our Core Ideology defines who we are. It includes a statement of Core Purpose, which establishes *why we exist* in the marketplace; our noble cause. It includes our Cultural Beliefs and Core Values, which describe *how we behave*. And it includes our Mission, which outlines *what we do*.

Our Core Purpose
~ insert Core Purpose Statement here ~
Our Cultural Beliefs
~ insert Cultural Beliefs here ~
Our Core Values
~ insert Core Values here ~
Our Mission
~ insert Mission Statement here ~

The first step of creating a roadmap to a compelling and significantly different Future State is to define our Vision of the future. Vision describes what we want to become. It is a timeless statement that is both aspirational and inspirational for our coworkers.

Our Vision

~ insert Vision Statement here ~

The North Star is our anchor in the sky. It is a landmark that helps determine direction as it glows brightly to guide and lead us toward a purposeful destination defined by our Vision and Overarching Goals. Our North Star depicts a beacon of inspiration and hope for *~insert organization's name~*.

Our North Star

~ insert North Star statement here ~

Our Overarching Goals for 20YY

The overarching goals set in 20XX created a verbal picture of what our company will look like at the end of 20YY. Achieving these goals moves us toward and embodies the spirit of our Vision.

~insert organization's name~:
1. ~insert an Overarching Goal for 20YY, written in the present tense, imperative mood~
2. ~insert an Overarching Goal for 20YY, written in the present tense, imperative mood~

3. ~insert an Overarching Goal for 20YY, written in the present tense, imperative mood~

4. ~insert an Overarching Goal for 20YY, written in the present tense, imperative mood~

5. ~insert an Overarching Goal for 20YY, written in the present tense, imperative mood~

Metrics – Key Performance Indicators (KPIs)

KPI s help define what success looks like and provide quantifiable measures of key elements necessary to achieve our Overarching Goals. KPI's are established *~for the organization~* each year. The KPIs create line of sight for all co-workers on key aspects of their respective operations that can influence progress to our Overarching Goals. KPI's are monitored and reported to *~ the organization~* on a monthly basis, although some benchmarks are based upon quarterly results.

Thematic Goal

Thematic goals help us tie together our longer-term Vision with our current key strategic initiatives by answering the question, *If we accomplish only one thing during the next year, what would it be?* For 20xx our Thematic Goal is:

~ insert Thematic Goal here ~

Our Key Strategies for 20xx

Based upon the foundation of our Core Ideology, the leadership of *~insert organization's name~* adopted ~insert #~ Key Strategic Initiatives for 20xx to fulfill our Vision and move us towards our Overarching Goals for 20YY. The specific Key Strategies and Definitions of Success follow. A separate one-page Traction Plan is maintained, defining the specific steps to be taken in 90-day increments to achieve the Definitions of Success for each Key Strategy over the next 12 months.

20xx KS-1: ~insert 1–2-word title~

Objective: ~insert one sentence description~

Definition of Success: *We will know we have been successful in implementing ~ insert title of the key strategy~ when, by xx/yy/zzzz, we have:*

    a.

    b.

    c.

Champion: ~insert KS champion's name~

Members: ~insert KS team member names~

APPENDIX 3

Definitions – *The Language of Business Success*

The following list of definitions are extracted from various portions of Recipe for Business Success. Definitions are derived from traditional dictionaries (e.g., Merriam-Webster), business websites (e.g., Investopedia), business texts (e.g., *The OZ Principle*), and the author's own professional experiences. Citations for terms from recognized outside sources are credited contemporaneously in the text and in the Citations and References portion at the conclusion of each Part.

Accountability: A personal choice to rise above one's circumstances and demonstrate the ownership necessary for achieving desired results – to See It, Own It, Solve It, and Do It.

After-Action Review: A technique for improving processes and execution by analyzing the intended outcome and actual outcome of an action, then determining why there was a difference and what can be learned from it.

Agility: The organizational capacity to effectively detect, assess, and respond to environmental changes in ways that are purposeful, decisive, and grounded in the will to win.

Aspirational Value: Those values that an organization desires or needs to succeed in the future but currently lacks. When defined, they help answer the question, *How do we behave?*

(Business) Success: Conducting a lawful, ethical, profitable, and sustainable organization to grow value for all stakeholders over the long term while embracing environmental, social, and governance responsibilities.

Catalytic Questions: Those questions specifically framed to help dissolve barriers to creative thinking and channel pursuit of solutions into new pathways.

Convergent Thinking: Creative processes or techniques designed to reduce the range of possibilities and focus efforts on the best-suited solutions from a range of options.

Core Ideology: The triad of core purpose, cultural beliefs and values, and mission that comprise the concepts and characteristics that guide an organization's culture.

Core Purpose: Describes the fundamental reason an organization exists. It describes the philosophical reason of *Why we exist* in the marketplace and *our noble cause.*

Core Values: Those values that are central, timeless, guiding principles that are truly believed and underpin an organization. When defined, they help describe *How we behave.*

Cross-Organizational Planning: Executives are joined by Influencers from senior, operational, and front-line supervisors and leaders in identifying overall direction, long-term goals, and short-term objectives for an organization.

Cultural Assessments: Tools and techniques (including culture walks, culture interviews, and culture surveys) used to study and characterize the culture of an organization.

Cultural Beliefs: Describe how people individually and collectively interact with one another to accomplish tasks. When defined, they help describe *How we behave.*

Culture: Represents the values, systems, attitudes, and set of assumptions that people in an organization share and adopt to achieve stated goals and objectives.

Definitions of Success: Provide the specific, measurable results that must be achieved to accomplish an objective. Definitions of Success for Key Strategies answer the question: *What must be true one year (12 months) from now, for us to be able to look back and say with any credibility, that we were successful with this key strategy?*

Divergent Thinking: Creative processes or techniques of generating original ideas and possibilities (e.g., brainstorming).

Execution: Involves having the right people required to support the organization's strategy and making sure they are efficiently doing what is most important to achieve those goals.

Facilitator: One that helps bring about an outcome by providing indirect or unobtrusive assistance, guidance, or supervision. In strategic planning, the key roles of a facilitator are to manage the process, manage the clock, bring about resolution, and focus on outcomes.

Future State: A verbal picture of the desired destination comprised of an aspirational vision statement and longer-range (3-5 year) overarching goals, and possibly a North Star.

Hierarchical Planning: Executive management with explicit responsibility for working 'on the business' identify overall strategic direction and long-term goals, while operational leadership identifies short-term objectives for their respective business units that are in alignment with and supportive of the long-term goal(s) identified by the executives.

Implementation Plan: A spreadsheet or other tool or process used to manage and track progress on specific tasks that must be initiated and/or completed in 90-day increments to move towards meeting the annualized Definitions of Success for each Key Strategy.

Influencers: People whose opinion and advice are respected and valued by many others within the work environment, irrespective of positional authority, including those working in differing business units and functions.

Intellectual humility: A non-threatening awareness of one's intellectual fallibility. An intellectually humble person finds the right balance between dogmatically rejecting the dissenting viewpoints of others and yielding too quickly in the face of intellectual conflict.

Intentional Servant Leadership: Intentional leaders define their desired outcomes, both stated and unstated, and anticipate the consequences of their actions, both intended and unintended. Servant leaders make a conscious choice to lead through service to others. Servant leaders identify the legitimate needs of their teams and remove barriers so others can be successful. When combined, the role of an intentional servant leader is to help ordinary people achieve extraordinary results.

Key Strategic Initiatives: Reflect the most important things to focus on in the short term (i.e., 12 months) that are consistent with an organization's vision and move the organization towards its longer-term (3-5 year) overarching goals. Key Strategies are comprised of a 1–2-word title, an Objective statement that succinctly describes the desired outcome, and detailed Definitions of Success.

Leadership: The skill of influencing people to work enthusiastically toward goals identified as being for the common good.

Leadership Practice: The actual application of and use of leadership methods and skills, as opposed to theories relating to them, through intentional incorporation of habitual exercises to maintain and improve one's proficiency as a leader.

Mission Statement: Describes how an organization fulfills its core purpose and vision. When properly defined, Mission statements focus on today and describe *What we do* while conveying the human emotion and motivation of employees and customers that buy into *what we do.*

Normative behaviors: Behavior patterns (norms) that emerge over time that describe how people actually interact, communicate, collaborate, and share; (unwritten) rules and standards that are understood by members of a group, and that guide and/or constrain social behavior.

North Star: An anchor and guiding light phrase added in the verbal description of the *Future State* between the timeless, qualitative vision statement and quantitative long-term overarching goals.

Open-mindedness: Being critically receptive to alternative possibilities. Being willing to think again despite having formed an opinion, and sincerely trying to avoid those conditions and offset those factors which constrain and distort our reflections.

Overarching Goals: Create a definitive and objective description of what an organization will look like at some point in the future, usually 3 to 5 years from the present, in the form of SMART goals.

Performance Management: An ongoing process of communication between a supervisor and an employee that occurs routinely throughout the year, in support of accomplishing mutually accepted and quantifiable personal goals that are in alignment with the strategic objectives of the organization.

Present State: Establishing a mutual, collective understanding of the current state of organizational health and the business environment through consideration of the status of current strategic initiatives, survey input, and various analytical data.

Plan for Success: Reflects the roadmap for going from the *Present State* (characterized by the SWOT Analysis) to the desired *Future State* (characterized by the Vision statement and Overarching Goals). The Plan for Success roadmap defines how goals are to be achieved and marshal resources (people, time, money) for their most efficient and effective use and includes Key Strategic Initiatives, Traction Plans, and Review & Reload sessions.

Review & Reload Session: A scheduled (usually quarterly) process designed to promote accountability, monitor progress, and allow for course corrections as events unfold.

SMART Goals: Specific, **M**easurable, **A**chievable, **R**elevant, and **T**imebound statement of goals that create an objective and quantifiable picture of the desired outcomes.

Strategic Envisioning: A systematic process of imagining future possibilities and providing notional direction to the strategic planning process.

Strategic Planning: An ongoing process that provides a roadmap for taking an organization from a well-defined Present State to a compelling and different Future State.

Strategy: The art and science of deploying resources (people, time, money) to achieve stated goals of an organization (i.e., enterprise, business unit, or product/service line).

SWOT Analysis: An exercise used to categorize internal factors an organization excels at that separates it from its competitors (Strengths) or needs to improve upon to perform at its optimum (Weaknesses), and external factors that offer a competitive advantage (Opportunities) or have the potential to harm the organization (Threats).

Success (Business): Conducting a lawful, ethical, profitable, and sustainable organization to grow value for all stakeholders over the long term while embracing environmental, social, and governance responsibilities.

Thematic Goal: A phrase added to the Plan for Success designed to rally employees around a common cause and to create an anchor or singular theme that unites all Key Strategic Initiatives.

Vision Statement: Paints a verbal picture of the future by describing *What we want to become.* When properly defined, it conveys an idealistic picture of the future to employees and other interested stakeholders, is inspirational – motivating employees to be engaged for the common good – and aspirational – a timeless ideal never to be fully realized.

ABOUT THE AUTHOR

Daniel P. Adley (Dan) is a former CEO of KTA-Tator, Inc., a nationwide materials engineering, inspection, and testing firm founded by Kenneth Tator in 1949. In 2010 Dan led a team on the first of two transactions to acquire the second-generation family business, helping it become a 100 percent employee-owned S-Corp ESOP. In the first ten years, values of shares held by the ESOP grew at a 22 percent CAGR, partially fulling the company vision of "security in retirement" for all co-owners.

Having earned a B.A. in Chemistry with Honors from St. Vincent College and an M.S. (with University Scholar award) in Industrial Hygiene from the University of Pittsburgh, Dan is a chemist by education and an occupational and environmental health scientist by profession. A passion for management and leadership emerged as Dan provided diversified safety and health consulting services, as he evolved from a student of strategic leadership to a practitioner and ultimately to a consultant on management and governance practices, leadership development, and strategic planning.

Over the past twenty-five years, Dan has consulted with organizations of all types and sizes on issues involving strategic and tactical planning, leadership development, governance, and envisioning future possibilities. Whether co-founding the Pennsylvania Center of Employee Ownership, serving as Director of Strategy for 35,000 member NACE International, or working with entrepreneurial start-ups and dominant mid-market private companies, Dan has helped both non-profit organizations and private companies define and achieve their highest aspirations. This book emerged as a compilation of the most important lessons learned from a combination of lifelong learning and forty-five years of diverse business experience.

Recently retired and working as a Strategic Advisor, Dan lives in the Charleston, SC area with his wife, near to their two adult children, their spouses, and six grandchildren.

RecipeForBusinessSuccess.net

www.ingramcontent.com/pod-product-compliance
Lightning Source LLC
Chambersburg PA
CBHW031843200326
41597CB00012B/246